DESMOND TUTU

DESMOND TUTU

BY DENNIS WEPMAN

Franklin Watts

NEW YORK / LONDON / TORONTO / SYDNEY / 1989

An Impact Biography

Library of Congress Cataloging-in-Publication Data

Wepman, Dennis.
Desmond Tutu / by Dennis Wepman.
p.   cm.—(An Impact biography)
Bibliography: p.
Includes index.
Summary: Presents a biography of the archbishop who rose from
parish priest to the highest rank in the Anglican church of South
Africa and earned international recognition, including the Nobel
Peace Prize, for his involvement in the anti-apartheid movement.
ISBN 0-531-10780-9
1. Tutu, Desmond—Juvenile literature.   2. Church of the Province
of Southern Africa—South Africa—Bishops—Biography—Juvenile
literature.   3. Anglican Communion—South Africa—Bishops—
Biography—Juvenile literature.   4. Race relations—Religious
aspects—Christianity—Juvenile literature.   5. South Africa—Race
relations—Juvenile literature.   [1. Tutu, Desmond.   2. Clergy.
3. South Africa—Biography.]   I. Title.
BX5700.6.Z8T877   1989
283'.092'4—dc19
[B]   [92]   89-31010   CIP   AC

The author wishes to acknowledge
the courtesy and help of the
Schomburg Center for Research in
Black Studies and the staff of
St. Mark's Library, the General
Theological Seminary, New York.

He would also like to express
his special thanks to:

Lynn Alison, Trinity Church

Margaret Larom, World Mission
Information Office,
the Episcopal Church Center

Henry Fuhrman, Office of Public
Information, Columbia University

Kathleen D. Treasure and
Dean James Fenhagen,
the General Theological Seminary

Bill Johnson, president,
Episcopal Church People for
a Free Southern Africa,

all of New York City.

Photographs courtesy of:

Bettmann Newsphotos: pp: 2, 64,
121, 138, 142 (all Reuters),
103, 110, 128, 131 (all UPI);
New York Public Library Picture
Collection: p. 16; AP/Wide World:
pp. 19, 73, 79, 94, 125;
IDAF: pp. 24 (Eli Weinberg), 50;
Impact Visuals: pp. 43, 63, 100
(Sue Dorfman/Atavia), 101, 116, 133
(Dave Hartman), 137 (Guy Tillim),
141 (Orde Eliason).

CONTENTS

DESMOND TUTU

*To all those who, like the subject
of this book, carry on the good fight*

❖ ONE ❖

"A COMMITMENT TO FAITH"

Riverside Church, on Manhattan's Upper West Side, was packed to overflowing that April evening in 1988. People young and old, rich and poor, black and white and yellow, filled every seat, and many stood in the streets. They were hoping to catch a glimpse of Desmond Tutu, the black South African bishop who had come to receive the Albert Schweitzer Humanitarian Award.

Thunderous applause rocked the air as the diminutive figure stood to accept the plaque and, before saying a word, walked down into the audience to embrace his wife and daughter. "It is a very great honor to receive this wonderful Albert Schweitzer Humanitarian Award," he began his speech. "At home, those who know me best believe—and I agree with them at least in this matter—that I do not really deserve the honors such as this one." Then he told a story that was circulating in his country. "When I died," he said, "I went to the pearly gates, of course, but St. Peter dispatched me to the other, the warmer place. Two weeks later, there was a knocking on heaven's door. When St.

Archbishop Desmond Tutu receiving the
Albert Schweitzer Humanitarian Award

Peter opened it, there was the old devil himself standing there. St. Peter, flabbergasted, asked, 'And you—what do *you* want here?' The devil replied, 'You sent Bishop Tutu down there. He's causing so much trouble I've come to ask for political asylum.' "[1]

The audience laughed heartily and warmly. This man from whom the Devil himself might seek asylum seemed far from frightening that night as he smiled and joked and thanked everyone for an honor he accepted, he said, only "on behalf of the many who deserve it more, the ones who are treated like dirt, as if they did not count, . . . as if they were things, rubbish, and not those of infinite worth created in the image of God and so to be treated not just with respect but with reverence." In that atmosphere of love and joy and devotion, it would have been difficult to convince anyone who had never heard of this gentle, humble, caring man that in certain quarters he was one of the most hated and feared figures in the world.

Since Desmond Mpilo Tutu was ordained an Anglican priest in 1961, he has worked hard for his flock, like any good priest. He has served congregations in England and Africa, taught theology, and held administrative offices for the World Council of Churches (WCC) and the South African Council of Churches (SACC). He was made bishop of Lesotho in 1976, bishop of Johannesburg in 1984, and archbishop of Cape Town, the highest-ranking Anglican churchman in South Africa, in 1986. Along the way he has gathered honors from all over the world, including the Nobel Peace Prize in 1984. He has also gathered more than his share of insults and threats. During his rapid rise from parish priest to prelate, he has never lost his simple demeanor or his pious spirit, and he has never ceased to devote several hours a day to prayer.

His enemies have accused him of meddling in affairs that are not his business, acting more as a political agitator than as a priest. But Tutu refuses to acknowledge a difference between politics and religion where conscience is concerned. To him, the South African government's policy of *apartheid* (literally, "apartness," the forced segregation of the races; pronounced, some say appropriately, "apart-hate") is a moral issue, and so it *is* his business as a churchman. "I want to declare categorically," he stated to an African newspaper in 1979, "that I believe apartheid to be evil and immoral and, therefore, unchristian."[2]

Increasingly, he has become a painful thorn in his government's side, a threat to the established order of things in South Africa. The white minority that controls the country has tried everything it can to silence this "pesky political priest." It has prohibited newspapers from printing his speeches and has more than once taken away his passport to prevent him from speaking outside the country, but he will not be silenced. He sees the very efforts of his government to suppress him as proving that he is right. "Why should they be frightened of one little black man who goes about saying a few things," he asks, "if what he is saying is untrue?"[3]

The social and political problems of South Africa go back a long way. When the Dutch, the first Europeans to settle in southern Africa, arrived in 1652, the native peoples they found there were hunters and herders and no match for Dutch rifles. Quickly subdued, the local people were driven north or made servants. As French and German settlers joined the Dutch during the next century and a half to establish a prosperous colony at the Cape of Good Hope, the native Africans were further subjugated despite a series of wars between the Xhosa people and the white farmers beginning in 1779.

In 1806 the English conquered the Cape Colony from the Dutch and in 1834 abolished slavery. The Dutch, known as Boers (literally "farmers"), needed slaves for farm labor, and 12,000 of them migrated north, in what was to become known as the Great Trek, from 1834 to 1854. They conquered and enslaved native Africans in battle after bloody battle as they moved north and into an area on the east coast called Natal. There, after a great massacre of the Zulus, they settled.

But the rich lands of Natal soon drew the English after them, and once again the Dutch had to give way. With numerous immigrant laborers from India, the English annexed Natal in 1843. The Boers were driven farther north and west, where, in the 1850s, they established two independent Boer republics, South West Africa (later the Orange Free State, named for the Dutch province of Orange) and the Transvaal.

It was not long, however, before the British and the Afrikaners, as those of Dutch descent now called themselves, were once again in conflict. The discovery of diamonds in 1867 and gold in 1886 brought adventurers and investors into the Transvaal. The Afrikaners resisted their interference until the tensions between them led to the Boer War of 1899–1902. This war ended in defeat for the Afrikaners, who were forced to accept British control of the entire territory, unified as the Union of South Africa in 1910.

*Workmen constructing field
fortifications during the Boer War*

Although the British officially governed the new nation, which included the former territories of the Cape, Natal, the Transvaal, and the Orange Free State, they allowed South Africa to elect its own government and make most of its own laws. The South Africans could not reestablish slavery, which was outlawed throughout the British Empire, but they created a social order as close as possible to what they had known in the old Boer colonies. From the first prime minister, Louis Botha (1910–19), the Afrikaners made it very clear that all power was to remain in white hands. Except in the Cape Province, where the right to vote was extended to those of mixed race—the so-called Cape coloreds—no nonwhite in South Africa was given a voice in government.

This fact has enabled the whites to maintain supremacy in every aspect of life and has kept the condition of the Asians, coloreds, and blacks, totaling more than four-fifths of the population, worse in many ways than it was during the years of slavery. In one of the richest countries on the continent, the great majority of the inhabitants are kept in desperate poverty. White per-capita income exceeds nonwhite by over ten to one. Education, free and compulsory for all whites, is neither for blacks (it is compulsory but not free for coloreds in the Cape Province), so few nonwhites would be able to advance above the most menial jobs even if good jobs were open to them.

Laws were enacted regulating where blacks could live and requiring them to carry passes, which they must show on demand, to control their movements at all times. Special areas outside the cities called *bantustans* (literally, "homelands of the Bantus," the Afrikaners' general term for black Africans) have been set aside in an effort to isolate the blacks. This has divided the country into one white state and a scattered series of small, powerless black states that occupy less than one-seventh of the country and include no major cities. These bantustans have the poorest farmland and no heavy industry, mines, or ports. The 40 percent of the black population forced to live in them have no legal rights outside, in the "white" areas, where they are technically foreigners, and may leave their reserves only with permission. They may vote for their internal governments, but they have no real political participation in the country at large. As one South African High Court justice observed, "The ballot papers in a bantustan might as effectively be dropped into a well as into a ballot box, from the point of view of real legal power."[4]

Political and economic domination by a small white minority has been a fact of life in South Africa since the seventeenth century, but as black awareness and pressure for more equal treatment have increased in recent years, it has become necessary to formalize white supremacy in a body of laws. Every decade has produced new and stronger legislation to control the black population. Under the third prime minister, James B. M. Hertzog, South Africa finally succeeded in freeing itself from the last restraints of the British Empire, which officially recognized it as a free and independent member of the commonwealth in 1931. The last limitations on the repressive laws it could impose were lifted.

It is perhaps ironic that the year of the Statute of Westminster, which created a free Union of South Africa, saw also the birth of a man who has done so much to rock the foundation of that country. Desmond Mpilo Tutu was born

*Students waving freedom banners. As
the black majority has increased the
pressure for equal rights and representation, the white minority has cracked
down even harder on civil liberties.*

on October 7, 1931, in the small gold-mining town of
Klerksdorp, seventy miles west of Johannesburg. It was
the custom then among Christian natives in South Africa
to give children both European and native names. Little
Desmond was born so frail that his family didn't think he
would survive. His parents had already lost a baby girl, so

his maternal grandmother gave him the middle name Mpilo, meaning "life" in her language.

The Tutu family was a close, loving one, although his parents were of different tribes. His father, Zachariah, was a Xhosa; his mother, Aletta, was a Tswana, and both languages were spoken in the home, along with Sotho, the language of Aletta's mother. Zachariah was a teacher, a stern, serious man who had achieved the high position of headmaster at a Methodist elementary school. Aletta had only a few years of schooling and worked as a washerwoman and cook.

Children were raised strictly in African homes in those days, and the archbishop still remembers how frustrating it was to be a child then. "[W]e had been brought up to know that children were meant to be seen and not heard," he recalled in 1979. "We were often warned not even to *look* at grown-ups as they were involved in some animated conversation. Living in cramped quarters, it was practically impossible to be interested in one's books, whilst people were laughing and joking in the same room. We were told to leave the room when other grown-ups came to visit our demigods, and we had to be quick about producing the tea (at any old hour) which the gods enjoyed guzzling in enormous quantities."[5]

If his father carried the strict discipline of his school into the home, Tutu remembers his mother as endlessly patient and gentle. It was her compassionate spirit that most influenced him as a child. He even takes after her physically. "She has a big nose, like mine," he admits. Aletta Tutu was a natural peacemaker, the champion of the helpless and weak. "She was always taking the side of underdogs in all situations, even when they were in the wrong," he told a newspaper reporter in 1983. "I suppose I either inherited or copied that."[6]

The people Tutu remembers most clearly as influences on his early life were invariably examples of patience, humility, and love. "I remember one wonderfully gentle black priest," he reports. "I served under him as an altar attendant. The thing I most recall about him is his thoughtfulness. He used to go out to the mission churches to celebrate Mass. After the service, everyone's attention was on him, as priests used to be treated like big chiefs in those days. But he wouldn't sit down to eat his dinner until he would come outside to see that we boys had been attended to." The thought that ran through Tutu's head, he remembers, was "I hope maybe one day I can be as gentle and as caring as this person."[7]

The Tutu family moved frequently when Desmond was little, as Zachariah was assigned to other towns in the Transvaal. When Desmond was about eight years old, he attended his father's school in Ventersdorp, where his classmates were blacks, Indians, and coloreds, but he felt no racial antagonism among the groups in school. It was only his occasional contact with white children that revealed to him that his race was considered inferior. It was in the school in Ventersdorp that he had to learn Afrikaans, the dialect of Dutch that whites imposed on the people as the national language.

A few years later, while living in Roodespoort, not far from Johannesburg, Desmond met two of the people who were most to shape his personality, and his life. His mother had taken a job as a cook at the Ezenzeleni Blind School, run by a white couple named Blaxall. It was South Africa's first school for blind black people, and the Blaxalls conducted it with such compassion and selfless devotion that Desmond was deeply moved. Mrs. Blaxall had found a young man who was blind, deaf, and mute, a triple handicap that under normal circumstances would have condemned him to total isolation. "She taught him how to understand English by feeling the vibrations and how to read Braille," Tutu recalled forty-two years later. "It was an incredible work of love; she had to go through the barriers not only of blindness, of deafness, of dumbness, but of culture. One of the sights indelibly impressed on my mind is that of Radcliffe—that was his name—standing next to the piano, tapping away to the music, listening— an *incredible* act of patience and love."[8]

The dedication to serving the deprived that Desmond saw at Ezenzeleni made a deep impression on him, but one incident impressed him even more. It was a simple, undramatic experience, but it has become a legend in his country.

The little boy already knew what it was to be a black in South Africa, to be taunted and shoved out of the way and to see his proud, dignified father, the respected headmaster of a school, publicly humiliated by white policemen, who would stop him in the street, call him "boy," and order him to show his pass. He had seen white children throwing away their free school lunches because they had carried better food with them from home, and he had seen his black friends, who were not fed at school, going through the garbage cans for something to eat. So his first encounter with the man who was to be the biggest single influence on his life, Father Trevor Huddleston, was something very rare and strange to him. As Tutu described the event many years later, "I was standing on a balcony with my mother when a white priest in a flowing cassock and a huge black hat walked past. Now for you it won't be surprising that this was so, but when he walked past he doffed his hat to my mother. I was utterly amazed! A white man doffing his hat to *my mother*? And yet, he was doing what was for him a natural thing, to be courteous to people."[9]

Tutu never got over seeing a white man—and so honored a figure as a priest—tipping his hat to a black servant woman. It was, in fact, a more fateful encounter than the little boy could have known. Father Huddleston was no ordinary priest, and the two were to meet many times again.

Trevor Huddleston was a pioneer in the struggle against apartheid in South Africa. Born in England to an upper-class family, he graduated with honors from Oxford University and then became an Anglican priest. In 1943, at the age of thirty, he went to South Africa to direct a mission and serve as a parish priest in the poor black slum of Johannesburg called Sophiatown. The dreadful conditions in this overcrowded cluster of shanties moved him deeply, and he began to speak out against apartheid and the poverty, disease, and despair it produced. He campaigned for justice so vigorously that he became the leading voice against apartheid and a major embarrassment to the white minority that ruled the country.

The government did what it could to silence him, as it was to do with Tutu years later. Huddleston's telephone was tapped, his mail opened, his personal papers confiscated. Once, when he protested the arrest of a schoolboy whose pass had been destroyed by the police, Huddleston was himself arrested. At last the archbishop of Canterbury,

Father Trevor Huddleston, a pioneer in the anti-apartheid struggle, had a tremendous influence on Desmond Tutu.

the English leader of the Anglican church, reprimanded him for getting involved in politics, and in 1955 he was ordered back to England. The prime minister of South Africa, Johannes Strijdom, is quoted as saying, "Thank God, that's the last we'll hear of him."

It was not the last the world was to hear of Father Huddleston, however. He continued his appeal in the United States and in England, and he wrote an eloquent book, *Naught for Your Comfort*, about his twelve years in South Africa. The book won an award and had a powerful impact on world thought. Perhaps the highest compliment it received was that copies that came into South Africa were seized and destroyed by the police.

But this was all still in the future. When Father Huddleston tipped his broad-brimmed black hat to Mrs. Tutu, he was still a parish priest in his first year in South Africa. He and the wide-eyed little Desmond were both just beginning to discover the realities of life there.

About two years later, when Desmond was fourteen years old, he became ill with tuberculosis and had to go into a hospital. He spent twenty long, lonely months there, undergoing painful lung treatments and trying to keep up with his studies. It was during this trying time that Father Huddleston's influence on the boy deepened. The priest visited him regularly once a week to chat, to cheer him up, and to bring him books. Perhaps Huddleston learned as much about the Africa he was coming to love from the bright, eager little black boy as Desmond learned from him. Years later, in a foreword to one of Tutu's books, Huddleston wrote of the boy he knew then as "full of energy and the joy of life," and said it was Desmond's "courage and patience that brought about his recovery."

For the boy, the effect of these visits was profound. "I fell under his spell," Tutu recalled. "There was this man, bubbling with life and laughter. He didn't laugh like most white people, as it were, with his teeth only; he laughed with his body, like an African."[10] But it was more than the humor of the priest that moved the boy; it was his compassion and his deep spirituality. They didn't talk politics, but Desmond knew that the priest was becoming famous for his outspoken attacks on apartheid. Here was a man who could combine a fierce dedication to human rights with a devout religious spirit. Father Huddleston saw the Church as an instrument of social justice and made no division between religion and politics. These long weekly talks must have planted a seed in the fertile soil of young Desmond Tutu's mind.

❖ TWO ❖

"EDUCATION FOR SERVITUDE"

Although the Tutus were a religious family—Zachariah's father had been a minister of an independent African church—young Desmond had no more idea of becoming a priest than he had of becoming a political activist. He was as lively and fun loving—and as ambitious—as any black child growing up in the sprawling, crowded ghettos of Johannesburg. Blessed with a naturally cheerful disposition, he enjoyed his youth and wasn't especially conscious of his family's poverty. His home was a warm and loving one, and Zachariah always managed to provide for them, although he was paid only when school was in session and had to work as a delivery man during holidays. Aletta supplemented the small wage she earned as a cook by taking in white people's wash. Between them, they earned rather more than the average black family of the area, and the family lived a relatively comfortable life. The Tutu home had three rooms: one for the adults, one shared by Desmond's two sisters, and the living-dining room, where Desmond slept. Like most of the houses in Krugersdorp, it had no electricity.

For pocket money, Desmond did whatever job he could find. He worked as a caddy at a Johannesburg golf course and sold peanuts at the train station. According to people who remember him from those days, he was a good businessman and always turned a profit.

Whatever his early ambitions were, the young Tutu was very serious about his studies. His father was a stern taskmaster who demanded the best from him, and Desmond demanded no less from himself. But he was not simply ambitious for good grades. He had a genuine zest for his studies (except arithmetic, which he failed one term) and pursued them with real interest. He loved reading. Zachariah, so strict in most things regarding education, was surprisingly lenient in one thing: He permitted Desmond to read American comic books, of which the boy accumulated a huge collection. Desmond never missed a chance to read American magazines of any kind and especially relished the black publications that came his way. "I can remember the day that I picked up my first tattered copy of *Ebony* as if it were yesterday," he told an American newspaperman in 1986. "The magazine described the exploits of one Jackie Robinson, who had broken into major league baseball. . . . I didn't know baseball from ping-pong, but . . . the most important . . . fact was that Robinson had made it . . . and he was black."[1]

Desmond was a good student, and when he began high school at the age of fourteen, he soon moved to the top of his class. Even the twenty-month interruption when he was in the hospital did not hold him back. With little else to do there, he read constantly, devouring whatever he could find. Thanks to friends, who brought him his schoolwork, and to Father Huddleston, who kept him supplied with books, he quickly caught up with his classmates when he returned to school. He graduated in 1950, as well prepared for the college entrance test as any black youth could be in South Africa. Only one-half of 1 percent of the black Africans who took those examinations passed, and Desmond Tutu's name was on that small list.

His ambition at that time was to study medicine, one of the few professions open to blacks, and he applied to the Witwatersrand Medical School. He was accepted with no difficulty, but the Tutus could not afford the tuition, and there were no scholarships available.

The government of South Africa needed teachers for its black schools, however, and it was offering financial assistance to young people who wanted to teach. So with his father's example before him, young Tutu decided on that profession and entered the Pretoria Bantu Normal College, a teacher-training school for black South Africans near the capital city of Pretoria.

Education in South Africa was completely segregated by race, but even in an all-black school there was some discrimination. The students were required to live and study in primitive grass-thatched huts called rondavels because it was thought that this would preserve their "native" culture and keep them from aspiring to join the white mainstream of South African life. The government-appointed teachers often made insulting racial remarks about their students, and Tutu and his classmates were subjected to constant taunting from the whites of nearby Pretoria.

Tutu's contacts with whites were not all unpleasant, however. He stayed in touch with his friends at the Anglican mission school, and Father Huddleston visited him at his own school. A classmate remembered how this "tall white monk sat on Desmond's bed" and how the other students "all marveled at . . . a white man visiting a black youth like Desmond and being quite at home on a bed in a rondavel."[2]

Tutu was deeply immersed in his education, but he was not a drudge and had not lost his sense of fun. His high spirits once got him thrown out of class for laughing aloud at a teacher. His lively, outgoing manner made him popular with the other students, who elected him chairman of the debating society and a member of the Students' Representative Council—two foretastes of things to come for the young man.

Tutu graduated from the Pretoria Bantu Normal College in 1953. With a diploma certifying him as a teacher in the Transvaal, he went to work at the Western High School, where he had studied. He moved back in with his family in Krugersdorp and went into Johannesburg every day by train to classes. At night, he worked on courses he was taking from the University of South Africa by mail.

The University of South Africa offers no classes; it is an examining body that grants degrees to students who pass its tests and gives correspondence courses to prepare them. Formed in 1916, it has a student body of over 50,000, who submit their work by mail from all parts of the country. Tutu studied history, sociology, biology, education, English, and Zulu with the University of South Africa, and in 1954 he received a B.A. from it.

With a teacher's certificate, a university degree, and a good job, the twenty-three-year-old Desmond Tutu was beginning to feel substantial and secure enough to think of starting a family of his own. Living in a home with two sisters, he saw plenty of young women, and he began to notice a special friend of his younger sister, Gloria. Leah Nomalizo Shenxane was close to the Tutu family. She had been one of Zachariah's best students and was now studying to be a teacher herself. Attractive and intelligent, she had the poise, warmth, and humanity that seemed the perfect qualities for a schoolmaster's wife. A third of a century of devoted married life since has proved her to have the perfect qualities for a far more challenging role: Leah Tutu has been Tutu's emotional mainstay through all the troubled and troubling years since.

Soon after his marriage, Tutu left his job at Western High for another one at a new school that had just opened in Munsieville, the black area of Krugersdorp where the Tutus had lived since 1943. The new high school was next to his father's elementary school, so father and son worked next door to each other.

Their styles of teaching, however, reflected their difference in generation and in temperament. The stern, dignified Zachariah Tutu was respected and feared, but the warmhearted young Tutu was loved. He was as much a friend and an equal as a master to the boys and girls, and they responded eagerly to his encouragement. Fluent in Xhosa, Tswana, Sotho, and Zulu as well as English and Afrikaans, he had no trouble communicating with students of all tribes and ages. (Some of his pupils, their education interrupted by the need to earn money to pay for it, were in their late twenties.) Tutu's own infectious enthusiasm made discipline unnecessary, and he never had the problem in his classes that the stricter, more old-fashioned teachers had.

An example of both his winning personality and his

personal courage is given in a recent biography of Tutu. A group of armed thugs broke into the school one day and began terrorizing both the faculty and the students. "There was a panic. The headmaster hid in his office, the teachers locked the classroom doors, and in Tutu's class the girls were crying, the boys rushing to secure their doors. Paying no attention to the cries of 'Don't go out, they'll kill you,' Tutu threw open the door and confronted the gangsters, who were as surprised as the students were frightened. For a while he talked to them, eventually managing to take the gun. Soon the terrified students heard the sound of laughter."[3] This disarming laughter was typical of Tutu even then. It has served him well many times since in confrontations more dangerous than that one in the Munsieville high school.

Tutu's life in Munsieville was relatively happy and successful, and he accepted its limitations without protest. "I didn't think [apartheid] was peculiar for a long time," he recalls, "because it was just how things were. You didn't question it." But he had never been blind to the injustice of his people's condition. Even as a schoolboy, he knew, as he put it, "that there was something wrong with the universe." All through his official education it was taken for granted that natives counted for nothing in their own country. His teachers had taught him, for example, that Victoria Falls, the mighty waterfall on the Zimbabwe border north of his country, had been "discovered" by an Englishman, who named it for his queen. "Did they really expect me to believe," Tutu wonders, "that none of the blacks who lived there had seen the falls until a white man came and told them, 'Hey, this is Victoria Falls'?"[4]

Such insults to the intelligence hurt, but there were

harder things to endure. Although he was a patient man, Tutu's forbearance was not unlimited. From year to year, he saw the situation of the natives grow worse, and at last it reached a point where he could no longer accept things as they were. The last straw came in 1955, with the passage of the Bantu Education Act.

This new statute was the culmination of a whole series of laws intended to keep the races apart. In 1948 the United South African Nationalist party joined the ultra-conservative Afrikaner party in a campaign for complete separation of the races. The word "apartheid" became a part of the political vocabulary of the country. Under the leadership of Dr. Daniel Malan, an ordained minister of the Dutch Reformed church (DRC), the government began to classify and register the population as white, Indian, colored, or black. Once everyone was registered by race, in 1950 the government passed the Group Areas Act, which required that all blacks live in specific areas allocated to them. This relocation often separated workers from their families, since wives could not accompany their husbands into cities where they worked. Natives were divided into small groups, supposedly along tribal lines but actually according to where it was most convenient to assign them to jobs. These groups were kept separate from each other to prevent the native population of the country from uniting.

The Bantu Education Act of 1955 was the most obviously discriminatory piece of legislation the South African government had yet passed, and as Trevor Huddleston wrote in 1956, "the most deadly in its effect." On the surface it is a simple and innocent-sounding law. It establishes no more than that the education of natives be taken out of the hands of the Department of Education and placed under the control of the Department of Native Affairs. But people familiar with the policies of the Department of Native Affairs understood what that meant.

The Department of Native Affairs was then under the direction of Dr. Hendrik Verwoerd, a psychologist who had vigorously supported the Nazis during World War II and whose racial philosophy was well-known. In introducing the bill in the Senate, he had made his position on native education clear: "The school must equip [the native] to meet the demands which the economic life of South Africa will impose on him. . . . There is no place for the native in European society above the level of certain forms of labor."[5]

The schools for blacks were accordingly converted into trade schools, teaching only the skills that prepared students for menial jobs. Class time was cut to three hours a day, and the per-capita budget for African students—about $12 a year, as compared to $210 for "Europeans"—was cut still further. If natives had found it hard to get a good education in South Africa before, they found it virtually impossible now. As one African writer put it, "Broom, pick, and shovel are the tools he must be familiar with."

At this time, the Christian missions were providing about 95 percent of the native education, and they depended on government support. When the new laws came into effect, the missions were told that they would have to submit to government control or lose their subsidies. Father Huddleston, who directed St. Peter's School in Johannesburg—one of the best schools for blacks in the country—was furious. He refused to comply and closed

St. Peter's down rather than participate in what he called "education for servitude." A month later, St. Peter's was reopened as a private school. It had no subsidy and had to charge tuition, but it was filled immediately and had a long waiting list.

Tutu had been teaching for little more than a year when this blow fell. To make matters harder for him, he had just become a father. His first child, a sturdy little boy, came at a moment of crisis in Tutu's life, but the young father was profoundly moved by the experience of fatherhood. Perhaps he felt some premonition of the spiritual life that lay before him. He later described seeing his child for the first time as "a kind of religious experience."

Tutu could offer no higher honor to his friend and mentor Father Huddleston—then in the worst trouble of his life with his church and the South African government for his outspoken criticism—than to give his new son the older man's name. In testimony to his love for the English priest, Tutu proudly named the little boy Trevor Thamsanqua Tutu.

A second child soon followed, a daughter who was named Thandeka Theresa. It is perhaps a sign of a growing sense of his African identity that Tutu placed his daughter's native name first and her European name second. He was to follow this pattern with both of his later children.

Tutu, his wife Leah, and their children faced an uncertain future, but the young father felt he had a duty to his people and to his own conscience. He could no more cooperate with the government in such a matter than Father Huddleston could. Rather than teach what he called "a deliberately inferior curriculum designed for blacks," he would take a step into the dark and give up teaching.

Tutu stayed with his class until they finished their course, and in 1957 he said good-bye to them and to Munsieville High School.

Resigning from the school system in protest effectively closed the door on Tutu's career in that profession, and he knew it. Desmond Tutu was twenty-six years old. He had a wife, two children to support, a teacher's certificate he couldn't use, and no job. He had to find something to do, and being what he was, he had to find something that would square with his sense of what was right.

Tutu had not yet heard a clear call from the Church, he says, but he had certainly followed one from his conscience; and perhaps that is not such a different thing.

❖ THREE ❖

"A LIKELY MEANS OF SERVICE"

Years later Tutu was to observe wryly that the Church had been his third choice. He had wanted to be a doctor but couldn't afford it, so he had become a teacher. Now he had decided he couldn't go on teaching and needed something else. "I looked around, but there wasn't very much else for me to do," he recalls candidly. "So it wasn't for very high ideals that I decided to be ordained, to go and train for the priesthood. It was the easiest option available to me as a black man. So I went to theological college at the beginning of 1958."[1]

In fact, even the choice of which church to dedicate his life to was the result of chance. His family were Methodists when Tutu was born, for no better reason than that his father was teaching at a Methodist school at the time. But when Tutu's younger sister Gloria enrolled in an Anglican school a few years later, the whole family became Anglicans.

The Anglican church is a worldwide body of churches stemming originally from the established Church of England but now independent wherever they are established. In America, it is called the Episcopal church.

Tutu had been a dedicated Christian since he was a child, attending church regularly and participating in the services. His association with the Anglican priest Trevor Huddleston had had a great influence on him, and now that he needed a direction in life, the example of that priest must have been a powerful one. As his father had been his logical model when he chose to become a teacher, Tutu now decided to follow in the footsteps of Father Huddleston—recalled to England two years before—and become a priest. All his life he had seen and been impressed by examples of compassion and devotion to others: his mother, the Blaxalls, Father Huddleston. It was typical, therefore, that he should seek work that would enable him not only to make a living and support his family but to live his life with meaning. "It just seemed," he explained later, "that if the Church would accept me, this might be a likely means of service."[2]

As he looks back on it now, Tutu sees the decision as an inevitable one, the carrying out of God's will. He was, he says, "grabbed by God by the scruff of the neck in order to spread His word."

Tutu has never regretted it. As he pursued his theological studies, he became more deeply committed not only to the practice of the ministry, the "means of service" he had looked for from the beginning, but to the spiritual faith itself.

His friends from school, and even his father, were not very happy with his choice at first. They thought he might have had a great career in education and that his intellectual abilities would be wasted in the Church. But when Tutu made a decision, he never went back. He applied to St. Peter's Theological College, the school Father Huddleston had directed until 1956. St. Peter's, in the Johannesburg suburb of Rosettenville, was run by the strict Anglican order called the Community of the Resurrection. It had the reputation of being the hardest and most thorough mission school in South Africa. It was called "the black Eton," after the exclusive English private school.

Tutu already had a more extensive academic background than most applicants to St. Peter's. He had earned a B.A. from the University of South Africa and had taught for four years in the public school system. St. Peter's welcomed him as a student.

Tutu's three years at school in Rosettenville were rewarding to him in many ways. He was popular with his peers—one of his classmates described him as "oozing love, laughter, and caring"—and in his last year he was appointed "Senior Student," representing the other students to the faculty.

When he enrolled at St. Peter's, Tutu had to choose between two courses of study. Along with only one other student, he chose the more advanced one, which led to the degree of licentiate of theology. The curriculum was very challenging, including Bible study and Greek. It was a hard discipline for Tutu, especially because his wife and children were not permitted to live with him. But he never grew discouraged, and he consistently got top grades.

Tutu gained much more than knowledge from his three years at St. Peter's. He discovered his true vocation— the religious calling—that he had not felt when he first enrolled. Private communion with God became an important part of his daily life. The schedule at school included a period of meditation before breakfast, and this was to become a lifelong habit. Years later he reported, "If I do not spend a reasonable amount of time in meditation in the morning, then I feel a physical discomfort—it is worse than having forgotten to brush my teeth!"

The ministry of the Anglican church has three levels: deacons, priests, and bishops. When Tutu graduated with an L.Th. in 1960, he was ordained a deacon and was ready to begin work on the first rung of the Church ladder. A deacon is an assistant to a priest, helping him in all duties except preaching. Tutu was assigned to assist at St. Alban's church in Benoni, another small town outside of Johannesburg. Here Tutu was at last reunited with Leah and the children.

The year 1960 was an important one for Tutu, the beginning of his real career. His third child was also born that year, a daughter to whom he once again gave an African first and a European middle name: Nontamdi Naomi.

The events of Tutu's life were exciting and satisfying that year. He graduated with honors from a prestigious school, began his life work, and became a father for the third time. But it was a dark time in the country around him. While Tutu was still a student in Rosettenville, social protest was coming to a tragic climax not far away.

Various organizations had been formed over a period of many years to protest the conditions of the natives in South Africa. The African National Congress (ANC) had existed since 1912, dedicated to unification of the many tribes in the country. The ANC hoped to secure by peaceful means equal rights for the black population of South Africa. But other groups were less patient. In 1959, some members of the ANC formed a separate organization called the Pan-African Congress (PAC) with demands for more sweeping reforms. It did not agree with the ANC that the control of the country should be shared on an equal basis between black and white. It called for "government of the African, by the African, for the African." Their slogan was "Africa for the Africans."

The ANC planned a peaceful demonstration on March 21 to protest the hated pass laws that required every black, male and female, between the ages of sixteen and sixty, to carry a pass. The PAC, wanting to voice the same complaint in a more defiant way, decided to march to police stations without their passes and demand to be arrested so that the law could be challenged in court on a large scale. The organization selected March 11, ten days before the milder ANC demonstration was scheduled, for their move.

That morning, the leaders of the PAC walked barefoot to the Orlando police station in Johannesburg and were quietly arrested, as they had planned. But other demonstrations were not so peaceful. A large group assembled in Sharpeville, in the next province, and waited for an announcement of the government's decision on the pass laws. The police became nervous as the crowd swelled to 10,000. Panicking, they began to shoot. As the terrified protesters turned to flee, the police continued firing round after round into the crowd. The 700 shots that were fired wounded 180 people and killed 69, including 10 children. A thousand miles away, another demonstration was dispersed the same way: Forty-nine were injured and two killed in Langa, near Cape Town.

The Sharpeville massacre became international news, and riots broke out all over South Africa. The white Anglican bishop of Johannesburg, Ambrose Reeves, denounced the government and had to flee to neighboring Swaziland. When he returned to South Africa, he was promptly arrested and deported to England. Also arrested was Albert Lutuli, the president of the ANC, and both that organization and the PAC were officially banned. From all over the world came messages of support and sympathy. The United Nations condemned the South African government for the shootings, and when Lutuli was released from prison, he was awarded the Nobel Peace Prize, the first African to be so honored.

The government of South Africa responded to all this with anger. It declared a state of emergency, making it legal to jail anyone on suspicion and hold him or her without trial. The press supported the action and denounced Lutuli. A Transvaal newspaper, *Die Transvaler*, called the Nobel committee's choice "an inexplicable, pathological phenomenon," and Lutuli was restricted to a small rural backwater, where he was forbidden to speak in public.

Tutu, in his last year at St. Peter's, followed the shocking news of the massacre on the radio. He was deeply pained, but there was nothing he could do. A penniless black student had no voice, no power, to influence the terrible sweep of events. He applauded the courageous Bishop Reeves, prayed for the souls of black and white in his agonized country, and devoted himself with renewed vigor to the job at hand, preparing himself to become a priest.

In December, Tutu dutifully assumed his first assignment, as the deacon at St. Alban's Church in Benoni, just east of Johannesburg. His superior there, Father Mo-

The police and crowds eye each other
before the shooting at Sharpeville that left
numerous people killed or injured.

koatla, was a stern old African who did not believe in pampering his assistants. He arranged to house the Tutu family—Desmond, Leah, Trevor, Thandeka, and, later, Nontamdi—in two small unheated rooms over a garage. Tutu's duties at St. Alban's were not all very elevated—they included washing Father Mokoatla's car—but he accepted them with patience, and he learned a great deal. He had his first experience of pastoral care, visiting people in their homes to comfort the sick and encourage the young, and he learned the joy of earning their love and gratitude.

A year as a deacon prepared Tutu for a promotion to the next level of the ministry, and at the end of 1961 he was ordained a priest. He was now assigned to a church of his own in the township of Thokoza, and at St. Phillip's he began to preach. The example of his former rector, Father Mokoatla, came back to him. He remembered the passion and power of the old man's speaking style and began to develop his own delivery, effectively combining emotion and humor. Tutu's warm, personal manner of preaching was soon to make him one of the most eloquent voices in South Africa.

Tutu made such an impression both as a student and a minister that the Church could not fail to notice him. Now thirty years old, with a brilliant academic record and a substantial background as a teacher and churchman, Tutu seemed a man worth grooming for a more responsible post. The principal of St. Peter's set in motion a plan to send him to England for more advanced study. It was an expensive project. Tutu had no money, and St. Peter's could not afford to support him, but so warm was the principal's recommendation that funds were obtained from several sources. The diocese of Johannesburg and the Community of the Resurrection chipped in; the WCC, which included the Anglican church, gave Tutu a scholarship from its Theological Education Fund; and King's College, in London, provided financial assistance. After a year in Thokoza, Tutu was notified that he was to go to London to continue his studies.

Tutu and his family had never been out of South Africa before, and from the moment they arrived in London in 1962, it was an exciting experience. Everywhere they went they were met with cordiality and a kind of respect that South African blacks are not accustomed to from the whites in their own country. Tutu could hardly believe the courtesy they received. "There, maybe for the very first time in our lives, we were treated as human beings by the authorities,"[3] he recalls. "We would walk about late at night—in Trafalgar Square, for instance—just for the joy of encountering a policeman, knowing that he wasn't going to ask for our passes. Sometimes we would approach a policeman and ask for directions, even if we knew where we were going, just to hear him address us as 'Sir' and 'Ma'am.' "[4]

The Tutus were set up in a comfortable two-bedroom apartment, the largest quarters they had ever enjoyed, and they quickly became adjusted to their new life. Although they were in a strange and very different country, the gregarious couple had no trouble making friends. Moreover, Tutu did very well in his advanced study of theology.

Part of the arrangement with the church that was financing his life in England was that Tutu was to continue serving as a curate—an assistant to a priest—while he was studying there. During the three years he spent in London working for his bachelor of divinity degree, he was assigned to another St. Alban's church, quite unlike the one in the dusty little black township of Benoni. This St. Alban's was in a middle-class section of London. The family became very popular with the neighborhood as they came to know and love the people of the parish. In 1963 the Tutus had a third daughter, whom they christened Mpho (pronounced UM-paw) Andrea.

Tutu's success as a student, curate, and member of the community was so great that his church allowed him to stay on in school for a master's degree. Because the Moslem influence in South Africa was an important one, Tutu decided to specialize in the religion of the Mohammedans, and for another year he studied Islam at King's College.

During that year, Tutu was assigned to a different church, St. Mary's, in Bletchingley, Surrey, a few miles south of London. Here the family saw a different side of England—the old, traditional life of the village—and it was a revelation to them. If life in a conservative English village was a new experience for the Tutus, a black South African family was no less new to the people of Bletchingley. There might have been some nervousness on both sides about the confrontation of such different cultures. Bletchingley was a very "high church" community, accustomed to orthodox services conducted in a reserved, dignified manner, and the outgoing, emotional Tutus must have been a shock to the people. But the encounter was a success from the beginning. The English were charmed by the warm African family. They chipped in to furnish a cottage for them; they paid to send Trevor to an expensive private school; and when Tutu received his M.Th. in 1966 and had to return to South Africa, they loaded the family down with gifts and gave them a large check.

Tutu was the first "overseas curate" that Bletchingley

had ever had, and his spontaneous, effusive spirit was something for which they were not prepared. Every two weeks, for example, he dragged his rector out, seated him on the back of his Vespa motorbike, and took him out into the country for a day of meditation and prayer—an experience the old priest resisted at first but came to love.

England in its turn revealed much to the African priest. Whatever he learned in his three years at King's College—and his experience there was a richly rewarding one—he learned more from living in that country. Above all, he learned to overcome the emotional insecurity that a lifetime under apartheid had instilled in him. "The most horrible aspect of apartheid," he wrote years later, " . . . is that it can make a child of God doubt that they are a child of God, when you ask yourself in the middle of the night, 'God, am I your stepchild?' " But now he and his family had lived with people who treated them as equals. "And so," he said, "we can walk tall."[5]

The Tutus returned to South Africa after a two-month trip to the Holy Land, and they were quickly reminded of what it was like to be a second-class citizen. To visit his parents, Tutu had to get permission from white officials, and once again he had to carry the passbook he had been so happy to put away when he went to England.

With a master's degree, Tutu was ranked as the most highly qualified black Anglican theologian in the country, and the Church was eager to assign him to a teaching post. He was sent to St. Peter's seminary, where he had studied. This school was no longer in Rosettenville, however. The government, more determined than ever since the Sharpeville massacre to divide the natives along racial lines, had made it so difficult for black students from outside the Johannesburg area to attend that the school had been unable to continue there. Other Christian schools had had the same problem, and at last the WCC's Theological Education Fund had organized a federal seminary for four Protestant denominations in Alice, a remote town in the bantustan of Ciskei in the eastern Cape Province. "Fedsem," as the Federal Theological Seminary is called, is made up of a Methodist, a Presbyterian, a Congregationalist, and an Anglican college, each more or less independent.

Tutu taught theology and Greek at St. Peter's from 1967 to 1969 and continued his own studies by correspondence with the University of South Africa. He was no less serious a student than he had been as a youth. He took his research seriously and worked hard with his students. But in Alice he had another duty that may have been even more important to him: He was the chaplain of nearby Ft. Hare University, a famous old Methodist school that the government had recently taken over. Tutu was a good teacher and he enjoyed the work, but by now he knew his first calling to be that of priest.

His two years in Alice as lecturer and pastor earned Tutu the reputation of a highly promising academic and theologian. He showed promise of becoming an important figure in Church education and was virtually certain of being appointed principal of St. Peter's one day. It was a prospect he could face with satisfaction and pride. But in 1969 he had an invitation to another school. The National University of Lesotho (then known as the University of Botswana, Lesotho, and Swaziland) offered him a post as a lecturer in theology.

It was not an easy choice to make. It would mean uprooting his family to leave his country again, since the school was in the independent kingdom of Lesotho, a small tribal enclave entirely surrounded by South Africa. The school, which had begun as a Roman Catholic college, was no longer affiliated with any church. It was an independent academic institution serving the three countries of Botswana, Lesotho, and Swaziland, and technically it was out of the reach of the South African government.

Tutu, determined that his children should not be subjected to the inferior educational system for blacks in South Africa, had placed his two older children in schools in Swaziland. As a lecturer in Lesotho, he would be much closer to them, and there was an elementary school connected with the university where Nontamdi and Mpho could study.

The racial tensions in South Africa had grown worse during the last few years, as the government responded more and more severely to any form of protest. The nation's schools were the objects of particular concern for the government. At Ft. Hare, which was a national school, student unrest had increased, as it had in universities in many parts of the world. While Tutu was chaplain there, it reached a boiling point. In 1968, almost the entire student body went on strike, and the police descended with rifles and tear gas to round them up and remove them from the campus. Tutu stood fast with the students, but he was helpless. The next day, saying Mass at St. Peter's, he wept openly.

In Roma, the small Lesotho town where the campus of the university stood, he could teach in an atmosphere free of the terrible pressure that was building up in South Africa; he could see his family live in the relative peace of a country without the constant threat of violence. More importantly, he could live with his family in a country without apartheid. He decided to accept the job.

For two years Tutu taught and served as chaplain at the university in Roma, continuing the life of the scholar and pastor he had found so rewarding in Alice. But he was not cut off from the world or from the problems of his country. He was increasingly concerned with reconciling the ideas of the universal Church with the African heritage and experience and attempted to teach theology from an African point of view. It was during his time in Roma— while carrying a full teaching load, acting as university chaplain, and continuing his studies in Islam—that he began publishing articles on "black theology" in religious journals.

Black theology is a movement that stresses the equality of mankind under God and considers religion from within the context of the human condition. Naturally, it is profoundly opposed to apartheid. Tutu was drawn to it and became one of its most articulate spokesmen. A deeply spiritual man, he came to realize that the purely spiritual life was not what God had called him to. He had to work in the real world to help bring about God's justice.

So, when in August 1971 Tutu was offered a job with the WCC as the African director of the council's Theological Education Fund—the organization that had helped finance his studies in England—he accepted without hesitation. Once again he had found what he had sought all his life, "a likely means of service."

Tutu at a Black Peoples'
Convention meeting. He
spoke out vehemently on
the human condition.

❖ FOUR ❖

A WORLD VIEW

Tutu applied for a passport for himself and his family in 1972 to take up his position in England. At first it seemed that the painfully reached decision had been taken out of his hands. The application was turned down. No explanation was given, but the government must have had its eye on the quiet little priest since at least his days in Alice, when he played so courageous a role as chaplain during the student strike at Ft. Hare University. It is not so surprising that Tutu might have been already considered a potential threat.

He decided to go to the top, the first of many times he was to make that decision. It was perhaps the only time it was really successful, however. Tutu wrote directly to the prime minister, explaining that his purpose in going to England was to represent Africa as associate director of the Theological Education Fund, a job that would, after all, help bring money into South Africa. The prime minister was apparently persuaded. Tutu got his passport.

It was, nevertheless, with no great certainty that the priest embarked on that long journey. Accepting the post meant giving up both the classroom and the pulpit. This was an office job that would require Tutu to attend meetings and write reports, far from the close personal contact Tutu had so enjoyed with his students and his parishioners as teacher and pastor. But it was undeniably a step up for him on several counts.

From a purely practical standpoint, it had several obvious advantages. The job was well paid, and for a man with a wife and four children to support, that was an important consideration. More attractive yet, it would take Tutu and his family back to England, where the fund was based, and that meant that his children could receive a good education and grow up in a climate of freedom and dignity. But above all, it was a chance to do something substantial, to engage directly in the work of helping others practically and on a large scale. It is perhaps from that day in January 1972, when the six Tutus stepped off the plane in London, that Desmond Tutu's career as a world figure began.

The Theological Education Fund was a young organization created in 1960 to provide scholarships for theology students in poor countries. As a unit of the WCC, it was interdenominational. It served the entire Christian community by training native priests of all denominations in countries that had no resources of their own for such education. It depended on missionary societies from richer countries for its clergy. Asia, Africa, and Latin America were its targets.

Tutu was excited at the challenge, so excited, in fact, that he set out at once the day he arrived in his new country to see his office and meet his coworkers. It was a small group—a director and four associate directors, each responsible for a different area of the world and each from a different country. Tutu was very much impressed. "We had some tremendous colleagues," he said later.

The director, Dr. Shoki Coe, was from Taiwan and handled affairs for northeast Asia. Working with him were Aharon Sapezian, an Armenian from Brazil, who worked with Latin America; Ivy Chou, a cousin of Chinese Premier Chou En-lai, born in mainland China but a resident of Malaysia, who dealt with Southeast Asia; an American Lutheran named Jim Bergquist, responsible for the Pacific area; and Tutu, who was to represent Africa. Tutu's colleagues were as different in temperament as in nationality, and they had lively discussions. When Tutu was asked years later when he began to develop his ideas about peace, he dated them from these exchanges. "I don't know how we ever agreed on anything," he said.

His ideas on black theology deepened under the influence of these men. The Latin American representative was involved with the related idea of "liberation theology," which emphasized solving the social and political problems of oppressed peoples. In South Africa, where racial injustice had existed for centuries, "liberation" and "black" theology were essentially the same thing, and Tutu was increasingly drawn to this approach to his religion. He had already begun to write for theological publications on the subject and continued to do so while working for the Theological Education Fund.

The idea of adapting Christian thought to the culture and experience of a people took many forms and names. The term that was then most popular was *contextual the-*

ology, which included not only the consideration of local traditions but also the conditions of life—the entire social, political, and economic context in which the religion was set. This was the ideal of the Theological Education Fund, to train priests from each area who would be sensitive to the feelings of that area. It increasingly came to be Tutu's ideal. The Church, he realized, could not exist in a spiritual vacuum. It had to be responsive to the practical needs of its members.

Tutu's job in England was not an easy one, but his life there was rewarding. In the first place, his family was very happy. The children attended excellent schools and were doing well, and Mrs. Tutu enjoyed the life of Bromley, the middle-class suburb of London where the fund's office was located. They even bought a house, an incredible luxury to people from a country where blacks were not allowed to own property. Perhaps more exciting to them was the chance to vote, another privilege forbidden at home. Mrs. Tutu was so pleased when the different political parties came to the house to ask for support that she would promise her vote to all of them.[1]

During the three years Tutu worked for the WCC, he traveled widely, especially in Asia and Africa. He visited Uganda, Biafra, Ethiopia, and Zaire—all African countries undergoing political and social upheavals—and came to understand the complexity and diversity of the problems on his continent. When Tutu returned to Bromley from these trips, he was eager to get scholarships for people in all the places he had visited. He often entered into frustrating arguments with his colleagues, who fought no less earnestly for their share of the funds.

Tutu found the administrative work exciting, stimulating, and satisfying, but he still felt that his first calling was that of a priest, and he missed the duties of a pastor. Although he was out of the country almost half of the time, he succeeded in getting assigned as an honorary curate at Bromley and conducted services at every opportunity. Like the parishioners in Bletchingley, the people of Bromley responded readily to his effusive spirit.

Between his pastoral and administrative duties, his continued studies and theological writing, Tutu spent a busy time in England. He was beginning to build a reputation for himself in the Church. In 1973 he was called upon to deliver a paper on theological education at a conference in Johannesburg and to organize the London Seminar for Research Study on Christianity in Independent Africa. His contributions to journals were attracting attention. He was growing personally as well, learning the delicate art of international diplomacy as he dealt with often hostile officials in many countries. More difficult for him was the art of handling money. Tutu had always had trouble managing his own budget and was often hard-pressed to meet his personal expenses. Now he was responsible for large sums and had to learn to calculate and distribute carefully. Problems with money were to plague him often, then and later. But he learned to cope with the demands of his work and was under consideration for the directorship of the fund when Dr. Coe's term ended.

Working at an international level broadened Tutu's horizon immensely. With the WCC he developed a world-view. But he was not yet wholly free of the narrowing influences of his life as a South African black. With all his increasing importance, he was sometimes still prey to the old insecurities. Tutu recounts an incident in the early

1970s when he got on an airplane in Nigeria and noticed that the pilot and the copilot were black. At first he was delighted to see black men entrusted with such important jobs. But after they took off, he became nervous. He began to fear that there might be a problem. He had flown many times before without worrying, but now he was uneasy. At last he realized why: It was because there was no white man at the controls!

It required a long personal struggle to overcome this nagging sense of inferiority implanted in Tutu by growing up in a country in which he was officially classed as inferior. "You come to believe what others have determined about you, filling you with self-disgust, self-contempt, and self-hatred," he explains. It was life in England more than his success at his work there that led him and his family to a full acceptance of their race. "We learned to grow in self-confidence and self-acceptance, not needing to apologize for our blackness, indeed to take pride in that which it had seemed wise to God to create us."[2] As the *London Observer* wrote, "When finally he returned to South Africa, it was as a man who had freed himself from the emotional and intellectual shackles of second-class citizenship."

With a life so comfortable, rewarding, and productive in England, it must have been tempting for the Tutus to consider making the move permanent, and perhaps they might have done so. But the Church in South Africa was undergoing changes, and in 1975 it called on Tutu to return to its service. Once again he was confronted with a painful decision, perhaps the hardest he had ever made.

When the white Anglican bishop of Johannesburg retired in 1974, some members of the clergy felt they should choose a native to replace him. The Anglican church had only one black bishop in all of Africa, and as the black membership of the church far outnumbered the white, it was felt to be time for another. Tutu was probably the best qualified black priest in South Africa. He had a high academic standing, he had published important work in theology, and he was experienced in practical administrative affairs. His command of modern and classical languages was extensive—an important consideration for an official of a large multiracial cathedral—and his ability to deal personally with people was legendary. Above all, Tutu was clearly a man of large vision, widely traveled within his country and outside it. Knowing South Africa but not limited to it, Tutu was a man whose spiritual and practical experience had given him a true world view.

A bishop of the Anglican church is an elected official, chosen by the vote of an assembly made up of both priests and nonclergy. When Tutu's name was proposed, there was considerable debate. Perhaps some people felt that he had been out of the country too long: four years of study and three with the WCC in England as well as two years of teaching in Lesotho. Others thought that his experience in administering education funds had not prepared him for the different task of administering a church. Probably there were those, too, who weren't ready to accept a black bishop, however qualified. After six ballots, the assembly was still deadlocked, and another candidate was proposed. The highest-ranking priest below the bishop, Timothy Bavin, the dean of the cathedral, was suggested. Dean Bavin, a white man who had voted for Tutu until then, accepted the nomination and was elected bishop. Immediately after taking the position, he asked Tutu to return to Johannesburg as his dean.

A dean occupies the third rung of the Anglican church ladder. The offer was a great honor for someone who had been a priest for only fourteen years and had spent most of that time in a classroom or an office. But accepting the offer would mean a great sacrifice. The family would have to give up the house they were so happy in, the children would have to leave their schools, and, as Tutu was determined that they would never be subjected to "Bantu education," they would have to live away from home. "My family and I deliberated hard about whether we should come back to South Africa," he recalls.

There was great pressure on both sides, and Tutu went on a retreat to think things over. He had gained so much from his life in England, did he have a right to enjoy that personal growth for himself and his family, or was his duty to his people to share his discovery with them? Mmutlanyane Stanley Mogoba, the secretary-general of the Methodist Church of Southern Africa and a close colleague of Tutu's, explained his decision in terms of national loyalty: "The call of the soil," he wrote, "became louder and irresistible."

But perhaps at last it was his children who persuaded him. "It was the children who said yes," Tutu reports. "Leah was very upset, but the children said we must go back."

South Africa needed him to speak for his people and to lead them to the pride he had found for himself. He decided to return—"to make a small contribution to the struggle," as he describes it, "to tell black people that they were people of tremendous worth."[3] It has been his message ever since.

❖ FIVE ❖

"THE PRIVILEGE OF A PLATFORM"

Desmond Tutu considers himself first and foremost a priest, but until 1975 he had had little opportunity to function as one. He was excited to return to his country and assume the duties as dean of Johannesburg and officiating priest of the parish of St. Mary's Cathedral.

He was the first black to hold this high office, and it was front-page news all over South Africa. Many white Anglicans were outraged, and a certain percentage of the cathedral's congregation quit, but the majority of the church was with him. His reception was very enthusiastic. When he was officially installed, more than three thousand people of all races, representing all of the many churches of the country, attended the ceremony.

Tutu's first personal choice was an important one. As dean of the cathedral, he was entitled to live in a large, comfortable house in Houghton, a rich suburb of Johannesburg. But the law of the country said that blacks were not allowed to live in Houghton. Since Tutu was the first black to hold the position of Anglican dean there, the problem had never come up before.

The Church had enough influence to make an exception for their dean, and it offered to get special permission for the Tutus to live in the deanery. It was a chance not only to live comfortably in a well-equipped house convenient to the church but to strike a blow against the Group Areas Act that prohibited blacks from living in white neighborhoods. Tutu refused the offer, however. He had returned to his country to bring something to his own people, and he did not feel it was right to separate himself from them in this way. He chose instead to live in the black township of Soweto.

Soweto (an abbreviation for *South Western Townships*) is a twin city about twelve miles outside of Johannesburg. At that time it had no electricity, few paved streets, and almost no public services. It was home to over one million blacks, most of whom worked in Johannesburg. Soweto was a little-known slum that the white population of South Africa preferred not to notice, but within the year it was to be in headlines all over the world.

When the Tutus chose to take up residence in Soweto, they made a statement of personal solidarity that won them the respect of blacks and whites alike. As dean of the Johannesburg cathedral, Tutu identified himself with Soweto further, working to incorporate the wretched black township into the cathedral's range of services. He pro-

Leah Tutu congratulating her husband on becoming dean of the Johannesburg cathedral

The sprawling shantytown of Soweto,
where Tutu chose to live as dean of Johannesburg

posed making free transportation available from Soweto to the church to make it easier for the poor residents to attend mass.

Tutu's contribution as dean was not limited to support for his black parishioners. He supported the controversial idea of the Church accepting women in the clergy and modernized some elements of the service. Like the people of Bletchingley, many members of his congregation were used to conservative, reserved behavior in church. Not all of them were as open to Tutu's innovations, spontaneous, emotional style, and effervescent humor as he had found the English to be, and his ministry was not universally popular.

Tutu's message—that blacks, like all of God's children, were "people of infinite worth"—was welcome to a congregation that was 80 percent black. Less so was the corollary position: that "whites, more than blacks perhaps, needed to hear that they are people of infinite worth, that they don't need to throw their weight about like a bully who feels hollow inside . . . ," as he recalled in 1986. "Once [whites] could accept their own intrinsic worth, then I said we'd have a bloodless revolution in this country."[1]

It was becoming increasingly clear to the dean that a revolution in thinking was needed in South Africa, however it was brought about. The conditions of life for blacks had deteriorated significantly during the past few years, and Tutu, living in Soweto and dealing personally and closely with his parishioners, was keenly aware of it. From the time of the Sharpeville massacre in 1961, unrest had grown more marked and more organized, and the Nationalist Party government had responded with ever harsher laws to keep the country under its control. In 1965 it had passed the 180-Day Act, allowing the police to hold people for six months without a trial or the right to see a lawyer. Two years later, the Terrorism Act extended the period of detention indefinitely. In 1974 it became possible to outlaw any political meeting. The Internal Security Act of 1976 effectively prevented the publication of any statement or news the government did not approve.

But the control these statutes were designed to maintain was becoming harder to enforce. Resistance was growing not only among angry blacks but among sympathetic whites as well. And support, moral and financial, was finding its way into South Africa from other countries. The ANC, which for half a century had tried to obtain justice for blacks by peaceful means, was outlawed, but it continued to flourish underground, and new, more aggressive groups had sprung up. Umkhonto we Sizwe ("Spear of the Nation"), a militant offshoot of the ANC, emerged to continue the struggle by means of sabotage and filled the native populace with hope and a sense of purpose. Umkhonto's leader, attorney Nelson Mandela, was captured in 1962 and sentenced to life in prison. His organization, however, like its parent the ANC, continued a vigorous life, and Mandela's influence over the years has grown, if anything, greater.

In 1966, Prime Minister Hendrik Verwoerd, the principal architect of apartheid, was assassinated, not by a black as a blow for racial equality but, ironically, by a disappointed white office seeker. Verwoerd's place was taken by Balthasar Johannes Vorster, a good Nationalist Party man who proved almost as inflexible an Afrikaner as his predecessor. Vorster had been minister of justice, an office black Africans consider a joke, and had been known for his stiff resistance to opponents of apartheid. During his twelve years as prime minister, Vorster bowed slightly to outside pressure by bringing about a few minor reforms—superficial changes like permitting blacks to use park benches previously reserved for whites—but essentially he held the line Verwoerd had drawn so clearly. (When Vorster retired in 1978, he was given the ceremonial position of president, but a financial scandal forced him to resign from that post, too, the next year.)

Tutu had followed his country's political and social progress closely all his life, but he had never felt he could do anything about either. As student, teacher, priest, and educational administrator, he had been helpless to influence things. Now, as a high-ranking figure in the Church, he had a voice that would be heard beyond his parish. He realized that it was his duty to use it. God had given him, as he said, "the privilege of a platform."

He began to attend political gatherings to familiarize himself with the complex realities of the situation. Beginning at home, he conferred with Soweto community leaders such as Dr. Ntatho Motlana, an activist physician deeply concerned with the violence brewing among the young people in his area.

Tutu also began to speak out wherever people would listen—not just from the pulpit of St. Mary's Cathedral in Johannesburg but in local meetings of social and political groups, black, white, and mixed. With Dr. Motlana, he tried everything he could to direct the bitterness and anger he found among his young neighbors into peaceful channels by organizing demonstrations. He addressed the South African Institute of Race Relations, warning its members that change was necessary if violent revolution was to be avoided. He was like a man trying frantically to defuse a ticking bomb.

There were those who felt that Tutu was stepping outside his proper role as a churchman, but he had begun to recognize the mission to which God had called him; he refused to be turned away from what he saw as God's will.

Then, in the midst of his busy life as pastor and spokesman, another major decision had to be faced. Late in 1975, after less than a year as dean of Johannesburg, he was called on once again to change his life. The position of bishop of Lesotho fell vacant, and Tutu was asked to become a candidate for it.

Tutu loved the mountainous little kingdom of Lesotho, where he had spent vacations and where he had taught at the university from 1970 to 1972, but he was not at all ready to leave Johannesburg. It would mean moving again, interrupting the work he had come to feel was the most urgent. Again, the decision was a complex one.

Many people felt that it was a sign of personal ambition—a serious charge against a man of God—to seek advancement so soon after taking on the duties as dean of Johannesburg. The congregation at St. Mary's Cathedral had grown to love Tutu and did not want a change after only a few months. And he had grown to love them, too, and to value the long-delayed chance to serve a parish spiritually and politically. "It had seemed the work God wanted me to do," he recalls sadly. "I mean that people had begun to think that perhaps I *might* be a pastor."

He felt, he says, "torn apart." As always, he sought advice from family and friends, and as always he made up his own mind. He accepted the nomination. If becoming bishop of Lesotho was not what God wanted for him, he reflected, he would not be elected. And if he was intended to receive "a platform" to speak out for justice, a bishop's throne might prove a higher, more influential one.

Still, it was with very mixed feelings that Tutu received the news that he had been elected bishop. It is reported that his first words were "Oh, *no!*"

Things were moving fast for Tutu, but they were moving even faster for South Africa. In all the turmoil of his forthcoming change of position and location, Tutu was still profoundly aware of the danger that confronted his country. He was determined to make a last effort to avert the tragedy he sensed approaching by going to the top, as he had successfully done in 1972 to get his passport. He wrote to the prime minister.

Tutu's open letter to Vorster (whom he addresses with the English form of his middle name as "The Honorable Prime Minister Mr John Vorster") reflected the blend of dignity and emotion, respect and determination, that characterizes Tutu's public speaking style. It has become a famous statement, much quoted and reprinted, and stands as the first important document of Desmond Tutu's public life. In it he outlines his position as a South African, a black, a churchman, and a man of conscience.

Since he was writing to a politician of South Africa, Tutu did not mention that he had already been elected bishop of Lesotho, but said he was writing as Anglican dean of Johannesburg ("and therefore," he reminded Vorster pointedly, "as leader of several thousand Christians of all races"). Then, shifting to a more intimate note, he assured the man he was addressing, "I know you to be a loving and caring father and husband, a doting grandfather who has experienced the joys and anguish of family life, its laughter and gaiety, its sorrows and pangs. . . ."

Tutu proceeds to point out how much more they had in common besides fatherhood: Both were members of races that had known subjugation (the Afrikaners by the conquering British, the blacks by the Afrikaners). More significantly, perhaps, he says, "I am writing to you as one human person to another human person, gloriously created in the image of the selfsame God."

He then makes a point that he has made repeatedly since: that it is illogical to argue that the blacks of South Africa belong to many different tribal groups, while the whites—"made up of Greeks, Italians, Portuguese, Afrikaners, French, Germans, English, etc."—are considered one. "Xhosas and Zulus, for example, are much closer to one another ethnically than, say, the Italians and the Germans in the white community," he notes.

Tutu dismisses the trivial improvements South Africa had proudly announced to the world in the United Nations: "It is not to move substantially from discrimination when some signs are removed from park benches," he argues. What blacks need is more than that. The reforms he calls for are clear: an end to detention without trial, the right of blacks to own property, an end to the pass laws, and "a national convention made up of genuine leaders . . . to work out an orderly evolution of South Africa into a nonracial, open, and just society."

The letter is respectfully worded, but the warning it contains is clear: "I am frightened, dreadfully frightened," it says, "that we may soon reach a point of no return, when events will generate a momentum of their own."[2]

Tutu's "Open Letter to Mr John Vorster"—running to some three thousand words, the equivalent of eight to ten pages of a book—was published on May 6, 1976, in the South African newspaper the *Sunday Tribune*. Within a month, it reverberated beyond the borders of South Africa. It was quoted widely in the press as a conference between Vorster and U.S. secretary of state Henry Kissinger approached. The British weekly *Manchester Guardian* reprinted an edited version on its front page with its own warning to South Africa. Desmond Tutu had found his platform.

Vorster answered the letter in June, dismissing its warning, according to Tutu, "as a political ploy, engineered, perhaps, by the political opposition." When asked for permission to print the reply, Vorster refused. He was not going to dignify what he considered mere propaganda by entering into a public argument.

The tragic consequences of Vorster's shortsightedness were soon in coming, and South Africa was once again in the world's headlines. Tutu had seen it coming in his own neighborhood.

"If the revolution ever comes to South Africa," a Cape Town newspaper wrote later that month, "it will start in Soweto." It was, in fact, in that black slum of Johannesburg that the violence Tutu had foreseen exploded. The growing anger of black youth there, dissatisfied with the Bantu education that deprived them of all chance to improve their condition, found a focus in the government's decision to impose the Dutch dialect Afrikaans, instead of English, as the language of instruction in their schools. Pupils at one Soweto high school went on strike about it in mid-May.

The government ignored them, and feelings mounted. On June 16, 1976, they came to a head. A peaceful march was organized, joined by students from school after school. Some carried banners saying "Away with Afrikaans" and "Viva Azania" (the name used for South Africa by activist student groups).

The crowd of black youth grew to more than ten thousand before the police panicked. A white policeman, without warning, hurled a can of tear gas into the crowd, and the students began throwing rocks. One white policeman drew his revolver and fired. Other policemen joined in. Soon all the police were loosing round after round into the throng. The first to fall was a thirteen-year-old boy, shot in the back as he turned to flee. Children as young as six were gunned down. It was, as someone said, "Sharpeville all over again," but on a far greater scale. Police admit to a total of 600 shot dead, mostly young children. Thousands were injured.

Like the Sharpeville massacre of sixteen years before, the violence in Soweto led to weeks of rioting throughout the country. Government buildings, shops, and trucks

Two young Soweto students carry the body of another pupil after he was killed by police in a bloody riot in Soweto. The high school students were protesting the mandatory use of the Afrikaans language in their school.

were burned. The police arrested many prominent blacks, including Dr. Motlana and Winnie Mandela, Nelson's wife, who were both held for months without trial.

The public reaction throughout the world was one of horror, and even the South African newspapers condemned the police. But Vorster was defiant. It was not a spontaneous outburst, he insisted in an appearance on national television, but "a deliberate attempt to bring about polarization between blacks and whites." He blamed "certain organizations and persons" (unnamed) for "working together to achieve this . . . with a view to attaining obvious objectives." His coming talks with Dr. Kissinger would not deter him, he asserted, from continuing to take firm action. "The maintenance of law and order is more important."

When asked why the police had not used rubber bullets to restore order, the justice minister made the government position even clearer. Rubber bullets, he explained, make people "tame to the gun." The *Manchester Guardian* concluded sadly in its June 27 account, "[T]here are few signs that Vorster has the will or the ability to place logic above the violent panic of his doomed defence." Vorster's only official response to the tragedy and to the storm of protest that it inspired all over the world was to appoint a "Commission of Inquiry"—consisting of one white judge.

Tutu was shattered by the fulfillment of his prediction. He was in the cathedral in Johannesburg when word came to him of the events, and he returned to Soweto at once to lend aid and comfort.

His open letter had appeared just a few weeks earlier,

and he must certainly have been one of those "certain persons" Vorster was later to accuse, but his position in the Church protected him from joining his friends Dr. Motlana and Winnie Mandela in detention. The government was probably relieved that he was soon to be out of the country.

Tutu himself was more divided than he had ever been before. Leaving Soweto in the midst of such turmoil—still very much aflame less than a month after the eruption of violence—seemed a desertion. But he accepted his destiny. On July 11, in St. Mary's Cathedral in Johannesburg, Tutu was formally consecrated bishop of Lesotho. A month later, he traveled the 300 miles to Maseru, the capital of that country, and entered the Cathedral of St. James to begin his duties as its bishop.

Painful as it was for Tutu to leave his country at that time, Lesotho was a stimulating and satisfying place for the Tutus. Desmond and Leah were alone now. Trevor was studying for a bachelor of science degree at his father's old school, King's College, London; "Thandi" was in medical school in neighboring Botswana; and Naomi and Mpho were both students in Swaziland. Still relatively undeveloped, Lesotho was something of an adventure for Tutu. His pastoral work took him to distant villages that could be reached only on horseback; the city-born, London-educated scholar, theologian, and prelate sometimes had to ride as long as eight hours at a stretch to conduct services. Nothing in Tutu's theological studies had prepared him to gallop through rugged mountain passes on the tough little Basotho ponies for which the country is noted.

The physical challenge of his life in Lesotho was, to a great extent, Tutu's own choice. He might have stayed in the capital, where he and Leah were close friends of the royal family and the international diplomatic corps. He had a staff of over forty priests who might have done the most strenuous pastoral chores more easily than he, since they were natives of the country. But Tutu always insisted on remaining close to the life of the people in his parish, and the parish of a bishop is the entire diocese, in this case the entire country. No part of Lesotho was too far away or too uncomfortable for Tutu to visit. He personally called on the sick and the old, conducted services in the prison, and traveled to the most remote territories.

Although the small kingdom had long been exploited by South Africa, the people of Lesotho—called the Basotho—took their South African prelate to their hearts. He was fluent in their language, which he had spoken with his mother and grandmother as a child, and he used it along with English in his services. His door was always open to everyone, and everyone was soon open to him. The close personal relationship between pastor and flock was very important to him. "When I arrived as their Bishop," he wrote for the *South African Outlook* in 1982, "the people said *ke nate*, this is our father. And they really meant it. . . . It was not just a convention or a polite title; they believed I was their father in God. . . . Every time it happened, I was filled with awe and a great sense of responsibility as well as joy."[3]

As always, Leah was close to every part of his life. In addition, she had her own work as director of the Domestic Workers and Employees Project of the South African Institute of Race Relations. This took her back to Johannesburg one week a month, where she organized educational and recreational centers for black workers in white neighborhoods.

Life was pleasant for the Tutus in Lesotho, but they were both still deeply concerned about their own country. They maintained close contact with it, and the bishop's public duties called him back often. One of the most painful occasions for a visit to South Africa occurred in 1977, when Tutu was called on to deliver a funeral oration for Steve Biko.

Steve Biko was the founder of the South African Students Organization in the late 1960s, while he was still in his early twenties. An important thinker and activist, he was one of the first to argue for an awareness of, and pride in, the black identity in South Africa. He inspired a movement called black consciousness, which was to have a lasting influence on African thought. Writing under the name of Frank Talk, he became a major voice for the young during his brief life and perhaps an even more powerful one after his brutal death at the hands of the South African security police. In 1973 he was officially "banned"—forbidden to talk with more than one person at a time—and four years later arrested and jailed. Kept for over a month, naked and in chains, in a Pretoria detention cell, he was beaten to death by the police. Steve Biko was thirty years old when he died.

Tutu was teaching in Alice when Biko's voice was first heard, and he felt its impact deeply. Not yet active himself, he thrilled to the words of this eloquent young man and knew him to be articulating the feelings Tutu was beginning to develop. Biko was not involved in the Church, but his words expressed, for Tutu, the divine will. "God called Steve Biko to be his servant in South Africa," Tutu said at the funeral, "—to speak up in behalf of God, declaring what the will of this God must be in a situation such as ours, a situation of evil, injustice, oppression, and exploitation."

More than thirty thousand people, black and white, came from around the country to attend Biko's last rites in his birthplace, Kingwilliamstown. They listened in silence as Tutu reminded them that Biko had seen "more than most of us, how injustice and oppression can dehumanize and make us all, black and white, victim and perpetrator alike, less than what God intended us to be."

Biko's message had become Tutu's, and over the slain leader's grave, Tutu gave it eloquent expression. The eulogy was, finally, a message of hope and faith. "Steve has started something that is quite unstoppable," Tutu assured the crowd.

The powers of evil, of injustice, of oppression, of exploitation, have done their worst, and they have lost. They have lost because they are immoral and wrong, and God, the God of Exodus, the liberator God, is a God of justice and liberation and goodness. Our cause, the cause of justice and liberation, must triumph because it is moral and just and right. . . . There is no doubt whatsoever that freedom is coming . . . . We are experiencing the birth pangs of a new South Africa, a free South Africa, where all of us, black and white together, will walk tall.

The coffin of Steve Biko, the black thinker and activist. He was beaten to death by police while in jail.

Desmond Tutu was a man of the church serving in another country, but there was no question now what he meant by "our cause." "Let us dedicate ourselves anew," he concluded the funeral oration, "to the struggle for the liberation of our beloved land, South Africa."[4]

Isolated from his country though he was, Tutu was becoming a national figure with such addresses as his tribute to Steve Biko. It was clear that he could not remain forever in the mountain kingdom of Lesotho. In fact, Tutu did not consider his placement there a permanent one, and almost as soon as he arrived, he began to prepare a priest who was native to Lesotho to take his place when the time was ready. He appointed Father Philip Mokuku his dean, and he began instructing Mokuku in the problems of the job of bishop.

Within a few months, in fact, Tutu was offered another position, a major administrative post. The SACC, the interdenominational contact group with the WCC, asked him to return to Johannesburg to become its secretary-general.

❖ SIX ❖

"A BEACON OF HOPE"

The SACC is an organization of twenty-two Christian churches that engages in many activities. It publishes two journals, conducts mission work, and sponsors programs of evangelism and theological education; it organizes commercial projects for the unemployed, provides funds and legal assistance to political prisoners and their families, and helps people forcibly resettled by the government. Its best-known and most controversial function, however, is issuing public statements of its theological position on moral issues. It has been criticized by the public and condemned by the government for many of its stands and has had numerous conflicts within itself about them. Its first major internal dispute was with the conservative DRC, which represents three-fifths of the white population of South Africa. From the beginning, the council favored equal treatment of the races, while the DRC argued that apartheid reflected God's will and was supported by the Bible. The difference in opinion was so deep that the DRC left the group in 1941.

In 1968, when the SACC took its present name, it issued a sensational pamphlet entitled "A Message to the People of South Africa," which declared the policy of apartheid to be counter to the teachings of Christianity. Prime Minister Vorster, a member of the DRC, as all South African prime ministers have been, saw the publication as an effort aimed at stirring up trouble. He blamed the influence of the American civil rights leader Martin Luther King, Jr. Vorster accused the SACC of "attacking" his church by dismissing its Biblical defense of apartheid.

The SACC refused to back down, on this as on other controversial issues. When they supported the right to be a conscientious objector and refuse to serve in the armed forces, the government passed a law making it a criminal offense to speak against doing military service.

The director of the SACC was always in a delicate position, and as the relations between the council and the government became more strained, it became more so. "The hot seat," as one of Tutu's colleagues put it, "had become hotter since the 1976 Soweto crisis."

Tutu brought with him some special advantages for this trying job. His spirituality protected him from the government's favorite charge of Communist influence. Since he is a South African, he could not be deported, as Bishop Reeves was. Tutu's greatest asset, however, was his own personality; whatever his official enemies charged him with, his infectious humor and personal warmth made it difficult for those who came in contact with him to oppose him. "Tutu could disarm the Devil," an American colleague declared.

Tutu began his job by getting to know his staff, and for him that always goes beyond learning people's names.

With each of his fifty or so co-workers, he formed a personal relationship. Blacks, whites, coloreds, and Indians—the SACC is as unsegregated as Tutu hopes his country will one day be—became his friends. He remembered their birthdays, attended their weddings, comforted them in their tragedies, advised them in their problems. Workers of all denominations called him "Baba" (Father), more as a mark of personal affection than as a title for a priest.

One of Tutu's first acts as secretary-general of the SACC was to set up a regular schedule of prayer for the entire staff, and every meeting began with a short prayer. He established periods of retreat for himself and for everyone who worked with him. At least once a year, Tutu still takes a personal retreat of three days or more for silent meditation and prayer.

Always a pastor above all, Tutu could not relinquish the work of a priest to become an executive. He applied at once to his old boss, the bishop of Johannesburg, to ask if he could serve in a parish along with his work at the SACC. At first he was given an opportunity to assist a priest, but in 1981 the bishop assigned him to a church of his own in Soweto. Somehow Tutu managed to hold down the challenging full-time job in his SACC offices in the heart of Johannesburg, keep up with the demands of a growing position as a public figure, and conduct the business and the services of St. Augustine's Church in Orlando, the tense neighborhood where the Soweto riots had begun a few years before.

Tutu's voice was heard beyond his parish, of course, and soon began to command an audience beyond the frontiers of his country. With the SACC as the platform he had been seeking, Desmond Tutu became a world figure.

His concerns were not limited to the problems of his own people. From his office in Johannesburg came a stream of statements on a wide range of international issues, officially representing the position of the council but sometimes expressing his own personal views. Many of his pronouncements were obvious—he called for peace and justice in Iran, Ireland, and the Near East, for example—and brought the charge that he was "simplistic" in his political understanding. Some, on more sensitive and complex issues, were controversial enough to anger people. He was accused of being anti-Semitic, for example, when he cabled Israel to deplore its bombing of Lebanon.

Most of the policy statements issued by the SACC, of course, were directed to the situation in South Africa. The council repeatedly condemned apartheid, detention without trial (especially of children), military conscription, army raids on resistance groups in neighboring countries, forced resettlement of blacks, and South African occupation of Namibia. The government had stilled almost all voices of black protest in South Africa. The ANC and the PAC had been banned, Steve Biko had been killed, Nelson Mandela had been imprisoned. Desmond Tutu, from the platform of the SACC, became the nation's major black voice for reform.

Tutu's impatience led him at times to level very strong and provocative charges against his government, which did nothing to ease the tensions or improve relations between them. In 1979 he described the wretched conditions of the squatters' camps where the Group Areas Act relocated blacks as South Africa's "final solution" to its racial problem—a reference to Hitler's policy of exterminating the Jews as the "final solution to Germany's

Jewish problem." The comparison of the government of South Africa with that of the Nazis outraged many people in Tutu's country.

Later that year Tutu angered the government even more. In a television interview in Denmark on September 6, he criticized the role of foreign investment in South Africa because "it is supportive of an oppressive system." When the interviewer pointed out that foreign investment gave employment to blacks, Tutu replied, "[E]conomic prosperity does not necessarily lead to political change. . . . We want fundamental change. We do not want our chains made more comfortable; we want them removed." As he continued, he grew more specific. "I find it rather disgraceful that Denmark is buying South African coal," he said. If the South African bargaining position were weakened by an international boycott, the government would be more willing to negotiate a peaceful solution to its racial problems.

"But if we do not buy coal, for instance, a lot of blacks are going to be unemployed," the interviewer persisted. "They would be unemployed and suffer temporarily," Tutu admitted, but it would be "suffering with a purpose."

When the bishop returned from Denmark, he found opinion sharply divided on what he had said. The chairman of the Christian League, a conservative church group strongly opposed to the SACC, accused Tutu of "sentencing South African blacks to starvation" and "trying to destroy the system of free enterprise." Even Tutu's friend Dr. Motlana, the Soweto community leader, admitted that he found Tutu's comments "surprising and puzzling." The government summoned Tutu to the capital at once and told him that his remark was "economic sabotage." The

(85)

justice minister said he should retract it and apologize. A few days later the minister of police and prisons publicly warned the SACC "to cease and desist from irresponsible actions." He suggested that the council was linked with Communists and accused it of trying to undermine the country, of "exploiting the unemployment situation" by setting up self-help programs, and of sending funds to illegal resistance movements. The minister of justice's reaction was simpler. "I'm disgusted," he said.

But the majority of black leaders supported Tutu. Two weeks after the interview, Dr. Motlana declared his wholehearted approval of Tutu's position, and at a public meeting of Motlana's Soweto Civic Association, Tutu was wildly applauded. The SACC backed him up completely, affirming his right to speak for the council. "Bishop Tutu has been called to leadership by God through his church and is, therefore, under an obligation to express his convictions," the SACC stated. "[I]f fundamental change is not achieved by consultation and negotiation, the alternative methods can cause a blood-bath in Southern Africa."

Tutu did not apologize, as instructed. Instead, he replied indignantly in a South African newspaper. He answered the ministers' charges point by point. "We know the tactics of the government," he wrote. "They plan to take action against the SACC and they want to prepare the public for that action." Tutu warned the government that they "must stop playing at being God. They are human beings who happen to be carrying out an unjust and oppressive policy . . . . But they are still only mere mortals. And we are tired of having threats leveled at us. Why don't they carry them out?

"The SACC is a council of churches," he reminded his accusers. "The Church has been in existence for nearly 2,000 years. Tyrants . . . have acted against Christians during those years. They have arrested them, they have killed them. . . . Those tyrants belong to the flotsam and jetsam of history—and the Church of God remains, an agent of justice, of peace, of love and reconciliation."[1]

Tutu was marching into the lion's den, and he knew it. As an American magazine pointed out, he was taking a triple risk: "He could be imprisoned or banned. Also the very existence of SACC—one of the few organizations where blacks maintain visibility among whites and also have a measure of protection—is threatened. Finally, he risks criticism from urban blacks who fear that boycotts would endanger their jobs."[2] But events proved that the risk was worth it. The SACC survived the storm Tutu's words had stirred up, though not without coming perilously close to disaster. Tutu emerged stronger than ever.

The South African government was clearly worried. World opinion was turning against it, and the threat of economic pressure was a serious one. The new prime minister, Pieter W. Botha, was a practical man. He knew he could not afford a direct assault on an organization as respected as the SACC, with more than fifteen million Christian members. But if this embarrassing council and its blunt-speaking leader could not be silenced, they could at least be muffled. On March 3, 1980, the government confiscated Tutu's passport—a warning that he was on thin ice. He did not get it back until January 1981, and he then immediately took a ten-nation tour of Europe and the United States to repeat his message.

The purpose of my . . . trip . . . [is] to see church leaders, government leaders and others who have influence in the international community to urge them to recognize that we are approaching a very serious crisis in our country, to urge them therefore, please for the sake of our children, for the sake of the children of all South Africans, black and white, for God's sake, for the sake of world peace, that they take action, that they exert pressure on South Africa— political pressure, diplomatic pressure, and above all, economic pressure . . . that will persuade the South African authorities to come to the conference table before it is too late.[3]

Three months later, when Tutu returned, he was ordered once again to surrender his passport, and for the next five years he was able to travel only with temporary "travel documents" that listed his nationality as "undetermined."

Lifting Tutu's passport proved a bad mistake for a government that was trying to protect its reputation in the eyes of the world. It produced a storm of international protest. The archbishop of Canterbury led twenty-four Anglican bishops from many countries in a formal condemnation of the action, and support for Tutu flooded in from American politicians and religious leaders. Worse yet for the South African government, it didn't muffle Tutu at all; the world press was all the more interested in what he had to say.

Tutu himself reacted to the move by becoming more active and more outspoken than ever. "If the authorities hoped that the confiscation would deter the fiery bishop," wrote an American magazine, "they misread the man." In one week Tutu urged parents to back their children in a nationwide school boycott, warned the government that there would be riots like those that followed the 1976 Soweto massacre if it continued its wholesale arrests of protesters, and predicted to the press that South Africa would have a black prime minister within ten years, "almost certainly Nelson Mandela." That same month, a colored minister of the Congregational church and former president of the SACC, John Thorne, was arrested for supporting the school boycott. Tutu at once joined a demonstration with his wife, Bishop Timothy Bavin, members of the SACC staff, and others and marched through the streets of Johannesburg holding a Bible and singing hymns. Armed police in full riot gear surrounded the marchers and arrested them all. Tutu spent that night in jail.

The SACC grew in stature and international esteem as it took increasingly defiant stands on such issues, but its internal organization suffered from a lack of attention. Arithmetic had always been Tutu's weak point—it was the only subject he failed in elementary school—and finances had always been a problem. The financial affairs of the SACC had been badly confused since long before Tutu took charge, and when he began trying to set them straight, evidence of serious mishandling came to light. Bishop Mokoena, a senior staff member from an independent African church, was revealed to have forged checks and pocketed church funds. The SACC wanted to avoid public scandal, knowing the government was watching for any opportunity to attack, so it preferred to handle the matter internally. But there was pressure to bring charges against Mokoena.

In court, the bishop claimed that Tutu had tried to bribe him to admit guilt and leave the country. When Tutu was summoned to testify, the court took advantage of the chance to discredit him. The judge, who acquitted the defendant, said that he found Bishop Mokoena "an open and honest witness," but said of Tutu, "His evidence cannot be accepted with safety by the court. His performance on the witness stand was vague, his answers evasive, and his evidence contradictory."[4] The national press reported the case with great relish.

A more serious attack on Tutu came about two years later when it became known that John Rees, his predecessor as secretary-general of the SACC, had embezzled more than $100,000. Rees was convicted of fraud, fined, and sentenced to ten years in prison. Some of the guilt rubbed off on Tutu and the council. Worse yet, Tutu had accepted some money from Rees under the impression that it was a gift from an anonymous German. When he found out the real source of the money—about $6,000—he returned it immediately, but Tutu still appeared to many to be implicated in the affair, or at least to have acted thoughtlessly.

The South African government had a more serious goal than just to connect Tutu and the SACC with individual scandals, however. In November 1981, the prime minister appointed a judicial commission named for its chief, Justice C. F. Eloff, to investigate the council's activities and finances. The five white members of the Eloff

Commission spent two years trying to find grounds for legal action against the SACC. Throughout the hearings they addressed the bishop as "Mr. Tutu."

The commissioners inquired closely into the council's goals to establish whether it could be considered a subversive organization, and it scrutinized the SACC's financial records. The council's books were in sad disorder, partly because of poor management and partly because the identities of both the donors and the beneficiaries frequently had to be kept confidential and were not recorded. About $10 million could not be accounted for—all from before the time Tutu took over.

The Eloff Commission was not a trial, and there were no specific charges brought. But the thrust of the questions was to establish whether money had been used to fund such illegal groups as the exiled ANC and promote civil disobedience. A recommendation from the commission could lead to bringing formal charges and a law prohibiting the council from receiving money from other countries. (About 96 percent of the SACC's $1,750,000 annual budget comes from the United States and Europe.)

Tutu was the first witness, and he made full and effective use of the opportunity. Here was perhaps the best platform of his life. The eyes of the country and of the world were on that small room in a Pretoria government building. Tutu pulled out all the stops, making the government inquiry into a forum for his ideas. A reporter for the *London Observer* called his testimony "probably the greatest sermon of the Bishop's life."

Tutu carefully outlined the tragic situation of his country, denouncing apartheid as a system "as evil as Nazism and communism." He denied that the SACC was politically motivated. It has a spiritual mission to realize God's will, he said, and this inevitably leads it to a concern about social injustice. Oppression is dehumanizing, he repeated, as much for the oppressor as for the oppressed. "When God encounters injustice, oppression, exploitation, He takes sides."

The white commissioners sat expressionless as Tutu spoke. "We are on trial here for being Christian," the bishop said, "and that by a government which itself claims to be Christian."

Tutu ended his speech with a ringing declaration of resolve. He was determined to continue his work no matter what the outcome of the inquiry.

> *I want the government to know now and always that I do not fear them. . . . There is nothing the government can do to me that will stop me from . . . what I believe is what God wants me to do. . . . I cannot help it when I see injustice. I cannot keep quiet. I will not keep quiet, for as Jeremiah says, when I try to keep quiet God's word burns in my breast. But what is it that they can ultimately do? The most awful thing that they can do is kill me, and death is not the worst thing that can happen to a Christian.* [5]

The South African press described Tutu's three-hour address as an "outburst," but whether or not the five stony-faced commissioners were impressed by it, the rest of the world got his message.

The commission published a report of its findings in 1984. It criticized the council's financial management and recommended that the government make it a criminal offense to advise other countries not to invest in South Africa. Tutu was denounced for his attack on military conscription and for his open approval of the ANC, but the commission did not go so far as to suggest that the SACC be banned. Tutu's reply to the commission's criticism was to reaffirm publicly his wholehearted support of the ANC and to renew his call for the release of Nelson Mandela.

Like the confiscation of Tutu's passport, the Eloff Commission inquiry did the South African government's international image more harm than good. Again Tutu and the council received messages of sympathy and support from all over the world. Invitations to speak came daily from everywhere. The government's attempt to discredit and silence Tutu only provided him with a higher platform and a brighter spotlight.

Honors had already begun to descend on the bishop's head. In 1978, King's College, London, made him a fellow, an honor bestowed only on its most distinguished graduates. The same year, the General Theological Seminary in New York made him a doctor of divinity, and the University of Kent, in England, awarded him an honorary doctorate of civil laws.

New awards quickly followed. In 1979, Harvard University added another D.C.L. to his growing collection, and in the next few years foundations and universities in Germany, Greece, Italy, Brazil, England, and the United States followed suit. In 1982, Columbia University paid Tutu a special honor by conferring an honorary doctorate of sa-

Tutu speaking at the United Nations.
He has appealed repeatedly to that body
to help bring about political equality
to South Africa's black majority.

cred theology on him in his own country. Since he had no passport and could not receive it in the United States, university president Michael Sovern determined to bring it to him in person. At the ceremony on Columbia's New York campus, a chair was left vacant, and President Sovern promised that if he wasn't allowed into South Africa to present the degree personally, the empty chair would remain a permanent part of Columbia's commencements. "Desmond Tutu is a beacon of hope and decency in a dark land," Sovern stated, "and we want to help keep that light burning. We want him to know that we care."[6]

❖ SEVEN ❖

"HEY, WE ARE WINNING!"

Desmond Tutu is fond of quoting the proverb "Distance lends enchantment to the view." It seemed that the more he was honored abroad, the more he antagonized those in authority at home. "Tutu's natural habitat is the American media," one South African newspaper reported bitterly.[1]

The African bishop's popularity in the United States did not, however, bring about the practical effects he hoped for. President Ronald Reagan agreed with him in principle, disapproved of apartheid in the American press, but refused to impose economic or diplomatic sanctions against the South African government. Reagan did not wish to alienate an important source of trade—the United States gets much of its gold, platinum, chromium, and other minerals from South Africa—or lose a strategic position on the southern tip of the continent. While officially opposing the racial system in South Africa, the American president preferred to maintain a policy he called "constructive engagement"—cooperation with the white power structure and the use of peaceful diplomacy to influence it gradually to dismantle apartheid.

For Tutu, it was not enough. Reagan's refusal to condemn the government openly and threaten economic pressure was a great disappointment for Tutu, who called constructive engagement "an unmitigated disaster." He angrily announced in 1983, "We find it galling that the leader of the so-called free world should be hob-nobbing so closely with our oppressors. . . . Blacks will remember that Washington collaborated with and supported a regime perpetrating the most vicious system since Nazism."[2]

For Tutu, neutrality from the United States was an immoral position. He expressed it in a favorite parable: "If you are neutral in a situation of injustice, you have chosen the side of the oppressor. If an elephant has his foot on the tail of a mouse, and you say you are neutral, the mouse will not appreciate your neutrality."[3]

There was little evidence that the interest and sympathy Tutu was arousing around the world was shifting the weight of the elephant, but pressure from within the country was making itself felt in Pretoria. In 1983 the country scrapped its seventy-four-year-old constitution for a new one that granted limited representation in separate houses of Parliament for the 800,000 Asians and the 2.7 million coloreds but still afforded none to the black majority of 23 million. Later that year, certain restaurants were permitted to decide whether or not to desegregate, and the law prohibiting racial intermarriage was repealed. Even so, the mixed couples who could now legally marry would still have nowhere to live in a land that strictly segregated residential areas.

Although the defenders of the new constitution argued that the government was taking a step toward dismantling apartheid, most of the public saw the move as no more than an effort to diffuse foreign pressure and make South Africa look better in the disapproving eyes of the West. As far back as 1979, Pretoria had been telling the world, "Apartheid is dead," but as Tutu noted, "Blacks say we have not been invited to the funeral." Such token "reforms" as the new constitution and later legislation offered did little to conciliate the colored and Asian communities and only added fuel to the fire of black wrath. New protest groups emerged to carry on the fight driven underground with the banned ANC, notably the United Democratic Front (UDF), a multiracial coalition of over six hundred labor, church, and student organizations opposed to the constitution.

Among the founders of the UDF in 1983 was Dr. Allan Boesak, a young minister of the colored branch of the segregated DRC and the president of the 70-million-member World Alliance of Reformed Churches. In 1982, Dr. Boesak had led the World Alliance to declare apartheid a heresy in the Christian faith—a move that the government denounced as "communist-inspired." Along with this influential religious figure, jailed ANC leader Nelson Mandela backed the UDF and managed to send a message of support from his prison cell. His wife, Winnie, openly joined the group, along with Bishop Tutu.

Tutu's days were full to bursting, his schedule crowded with many claims on his time. The affairs of the SACC, now under great pressure, continued to occupy him full time, the Eloff Commission continued to harass him, and his own parish in Soweto required his attention. But he always found an hour for prayer, and he never failed to lend his voice to the cause of justice when he could. In 1984, Tutu received an invitation that he could not resist,

*A vocal opponent of apartheid, Dr. Allan Boesak
is a "colored" South African clergyman.*

Perhaps the best-known South African dissident is Nelson Mandela. He has spent twenty-six years in jail for his views on apartheid.

even though it would require a long absence from his country. It was a call to return to his first work, teaching, at the General Theological Seminary in New York City.

Tutu's relation with the Anglican seminary in New York was an old and special one. They had given him his first honorary degree in 1978 and at the same time invited him to take the newly established chair of Anglican studies. He regretfully had to refuse the offer then because he could not get permission to travel, but the New York school had kept the position open and had maintained close contact with him. When his government relented in 1984, Tutu could not pass up the opportunity. In September he began a three-month assignment to teach "Contemporary Ecclesiology," described as "The Church and Its Response to Oppression and Injustice, with Particular Reference to South Africa Today."

His students found him fascinating not only because he brought them firsthand information about a country in the news but because of the unique magnetism of the man himself. "He spoke to the heart," one of his students recalls. "He spoke from within himself. His theology came from his faith, his prayer life. His main theme was his faith, that nothing could interfere with God's plan." A colleague on the teaching staff remembered him as "very huggable—he enjoyed hugging, and people enjoyed hugging him. For all of us here, he was a figure of great heroism and dignity, but he never gave the impression that he considered himself extraordinary. He made us all feel that we could be like him."

It was in October, a month into his school term, that the news came that Desmond Tutu had won the 1984 Nobel Peace Prize. The report caused a sensation on the campus

*Tutu and his wife hold a press conference
after it was announced that he had won the
Nobel Peace Prize in 1984 for his crusade
against South Africa's segregation system.*

of the General Theological Seminary. The chapel bells began to send the message far and wide and rang for twenty minutes. Tutu's first words were "Hey, we are winning! Justice is going to win!"

A great joy spread through the community, not only in the Anglican seminary but throughout the city. People flooded to the school's grounds from all over Manhattan to share Tutu's triumph. Dean James Fenhagen of the seminary led a group—the number swelled to more than two hundred—of students and faculty in a march to the South African consulate, "to bear witness." The crowd formed an orderly procession and stood before the gates in prayer. It was, in the dean's words, "an act of intercession for justice, for healing."

The award catapulted Tutu into such celebrity that he was pursued everywhere. He took calls from world leaders and movie stars as well as thousands of unknown well-wishers, and he had a word for everyone. He found time for interviews with schoolchildren between an endless round of press conferences, television shows, and public speeches. At every opportunity he reiterated his message. He blasted his government's efforts at projecting an image of improved social conditions in South Africa. "If things are changing," he said, "they are changing for the worse." He dismissed the slight concessions made to coloreds and Asians while still excluding blacks and warned that if real social change did not take place soon, "the bloodbath will be inevitable."

The award, he said, was for his people, and he intended to put most of the $192,000 that went with it into a scholarship fund for South African blacks.

Tutu and his family returned to Johannesburg soon after the announcement to celebrate the award with the people he felt it chiefly concerned. His reception was riotous. Hundreds of his friends and colleagues were waiting at the airport with banners reading "Welcome Baba" and "Apartheid Goodbye," and the police gave up trying to maintain order as the crowd cheered and sang.

Church leaders recognized the Nobel Prize as international recognition not only for Tutu but for the part the Christian churches were playing in the struggle against apartheid. They were delighted to see the spotlight focused on their country and its problems. The SACC announced, "The award to Bishop Tutu is also an award to the Churches of South Africa." Allan Boesak, speaking for both the World Alliance of Reformed Churches and the UDF, said, "What [Tutu] represents . . . has been given a tremendous boost by the award. I hope this will help bring even better understanding in the international community about the situation in our country and . . . our struggle for peace, freedom, and justice."

The ANC sent word from its headquarters in exile that it was "proud of our motherland's son" for winning the peace prize, though it reaffirmed its commitment to armed struggle.

The response to the honor Tutu received was not all positive, however. Not surprisingly, the South African government maintained what one Cape Town newspaper called "a stony silence." The office of Pieter Botha (promoted from prime minister to "State President" by the new constitution) responded to reporters with a surly "No comment."

The national press was not so restrained. While some newspapers, such as the *Cape Times*, openly applauded Tutu for the honor he had won and acknowledged him as a force for peaceful change in a potentially explosive situation, others echoed the press of twenty-four years earlier, when the only other South African winner of the prize—the antiapartheid leader and founder of the ANC, Albert Lutuli—was violently condemned. Many newspapers charged that a peace prize was inappropriate for a man who stirred up so much trouble. Tutu was condemned for advocating foreign disinvestment, predicting violence, and comparing his country with Nazi Germany.

The impulsive bishop was accustomed to official disapproval of his sometimes undiplomatic remarks, but he was probably more hurt by the response of some of his own people. Since he first spoke out in his letter to Vorster in 1976, he had walked a tightrope between militant radicals who considered him "soft" and conservatives who saw him as a dangerous revolutionary. White novelist Alan Paton, whose courageous novel *Cry, the Beloved Country* has become a classic indictment of apartheid, sent off an open letter to the Cape Town *Sunday Times* saying, "I have never won a prize like that. I am afraid my skin is not the right color."

Paton grudgingly congratulated Tutu on the honor but expressed his strong disapproval of the Nobel committee for interfering in South African affairs by choosing him for it. A pioneer spokesman for social justice in his country who had suffered some of the same official harassment as Tutu, Paton firmly disagreed with the bishop on the subject of foreign disinvestment. Paton believed that anything that damaged the South African economy would only bring further hardship to the workers. He felt that Tutu's position on the subject was both wrongheaded and immoral. "I do not understand how your Christian conscience allows you to advocate disinvestment," he wrote to the bishop. "I do not understand how you can put a man out of work for a high moral principal."[4]

Others who supported Tutu's social goals without agreeing about foreign economic sanctions were more cordial. President Ronald Reagan sent a telegram of congratulations, and so did Helen Suzman, a white member of the South African Parliament who had long condemned apartheid but vigorously opposed disinvestment as a means of ending it.

With the applause of Pope John Paul II, the Anglican archbishops of Canterbury and Cape Town, Nelson Mandela, Coretta Scott King, Indian prime minister Indira Gandhi, West German chancellor Willy Brandt, Polish union leader Lech Walesa (the previous year's Nobel laureate), and thousands of strangers from around the world ringing in his ears from one side and the condemnation of his government and many of his countrymen from the other, Tutu returned to the United States to finish his job at the seminary. Still the man of the hour, he had a hard time fitting into his classroom schedule the many demands made on him for speeches and interviews, but his colleagues there report that he always got to class on time and never missed one.

Tutu took full advantage of his platform during those last days in America. He spoke constantly, hammering home his points again and again, all over the country.

"Here I sit," he told one television interviewer, "a bishop in the Church of God, regarded by at least one or two people as reasonably responsible, and yet I do not have a vote. I am rising fifty-three years of age, and yet an eighteen-year-old will vote in South Africa because he or she has what we consider to be a biological irrevelance—a white skin."

Receiving an honorary D.C.L. from Howard University in Washington, D.C., Tutu repeated his conviction that constructive engagement is "an unmitigated disaster for blacks," adding that the recent abstention by the United States in a vote by the UN Security Council to condemn South Africa indicated to his countrymen that the United States thought they were "expendable." During this speech he recounted a story he had told often and could never forget. In 1979 he was visiting one of the "resettlement camps" where, as he described it, "blacks are dumped like potatoes after being removed from the urban areas," and spoke to a little girl.

"Does your mother get a pension or grant?"

"No."

"Then what do you do for food?"

"We borrow food."

"Have you ever returned any of the food you have borrowed?"

"No."

"What do you do when you can't borrow food?"

"We drink water to fill our stomachs."

"This," Tutu points out, "in a country which exports food! . . . That girl at the settlement will always haunt me."

In December, Tutu had a chance to carry his protest

to the top. It was an election year, and President Reagan did not want to antagonize anyone. He invited Tutu to the White House.

When the president's representative called the seminary in New York to make the arrangements, he explained that Tutu had to appear in the president's office alone, because White House protocol did not permit wives to attend such meetings. "My wife has been with me through everything," Tutu replied, "and she will come with me there, too." The official said he was sorry but it was impossible. "Look," Tutu retorted into the telephone, "the president may love his country, but tell him I love my wife." The White House spokesman hesitated a moment. At last he said, "Well, we might break protocol this time." Leah Tutu accompanied her husband.

The meeting took place on December 7, 1984, the day after thirty-five members of Congress said they would support economic and diplomatic sanctions against South Africa unless steps were taken to bring apartheid to an end. The President, however, made it clear that he had not changed his mind. He repeated his belief in constructive engagement and declared that the United States was going to continue with it. "We are no nearer each other than before," Tutu reported sadly to the press after the meeting.

During all this political activity, Tutu's career was taking another turn. The bishop of Johannesburg, Timothy Bavin, was reassigned to a position in England, and Tutu's name was proposed for the post. The bishop of Johannesburg is the spiritual leader of the largest Anglican diocese in South Africa, with 300,000 members, second in influence only to the archbishop of Cape Town.

It was a controversial nomination. Tutu was certainly the best-known Anglican in South Africa and highly admired for his ability, but he was considered by many to be more a political agitator than a clergyman. Some people felt that he would widen the rift between the church and the government. Others thought that he would be more useful to the church in his role as secretary general of the SACC. Some whites simply were not ready for a black man on the throne of St. Mary's Cathedral. The 213-member assembly of electors debated for weeks but remained deadlocked along racial lines.

At last the church's twelve black and eleven white bishops had to decide the issue. On November 3, 1984, they announced that Desmond Tutu had been elected the first black bishop of Johannesburg.

In a 1984 sermon delivered in a Washington, D.C., church, Bishop Tutu said he doubted whether his black countrymen could take another four years of "constructive engagement" from the United States. This was the former Reagan administration's policy of cooperating with the white power structure and the use of peaceful diplomacy to influence gradual dismantling of apartheid.

Tutu was sorry that he had not received a victory in the assembly, which consisted of an equal number of priests and laymen of the Johannesburg diocese, but he welcomed the new job. "The time is just right for me to leave the South African Council of Churches," he stated. "I am fundamentally a pastor. That is what God ordained for me to do."

Leah Tutu was glad the hectic events of the past few weeks were coming to an end. It was time to leave, she declared. Too many things were happening.

Three days after his meeting with President Reagan, Tutu and his family were in Oslo to receive the Nobel Peace Prize. They were welcomed enthusiastically. Students staged a huge torchlight procession, and labor unions arranged a folk concert for them. During the ceremonial dinner at which the gold medal was officially presented, word came that someone had planted a bomb in the hall. The room was evacuated, and the bishop stood outside in the cold Norwegian night as police searched the hall, but he was undaunted. "This just shows how desperate our enemies have become," he said with a smile.

When the dinner was resumed (there was no bomb, after all), the whole crowd was more joyous than ever, and the evening ended with the South African visitors singing songs of their own country.

Tutu's three-month stay in New York had come to an end, and it had been full enough. He was ready to go home and take up his work again.

Conditions had worsened in South Africa—there were strikes and riots and boycotts—but Tutu's faith in the future was renewed. While at the seminary he had received a letter from a man who said that he lived alone in the woods in California and prayed for Tutu every morning at 2:00 A.M. The bishop has never doubted the power of prayer. "I'm being prayed for at two A.M. in the woods in California!" he crowed to a group at the seminary. "What chance does the South African government have?"

❖ EICHT ❖

"MADE FOR FREEDOM"

The Tutus returned to a South Africa more divided than ever, and the conflict within the country was not a simple one. Violence had broken out on many fronts, not only black against white but black against black and against Indian.

Relations between the native and the Indian communities had long been strained, and the slight representation the Indians had won in the new government was resented by blacks, who still had none. Clashes between the two groups had become increasingly frequent as blacks vented their rage on Indian shopowners whom they saw as exploiting them and Indians organized raids against blacks for revenge.

The situation was aggravated by conflicts among several rival black groups. The UDF (representing the exiled ANC) was only one of the native organizations in the struggle against apartheid. Chief Mangosuthu Gatsha Buthelezi, the leader of the country's 6 million Zulus, is the founder of Inkatha, an organization of over a million members. Like Tutu, he is considered a moderate, and he has always

*Tutu presents his Nobel Prize
to the people of Soweto.*

opposed violence in his pursuit of social reform, but his army of "Inkis" are blamed for much of South Africa's intertribal terrorism. Inkatha and the ANC have long been at odds, each blaming the other for outbreaks of violence among blacks. Buthelezi is a skilled politician who heads KwaZulu, the largest of the nation's ten tribal homelands, and an influential voice in the country. He has called Tutu a hypocrite for claiming to be opposed to violence and yet openly supporting the militant ANC. Although he shares Tutu's goal of a peaceful solution to the country's problems, he firmly opposes disinvestment and is naturally much more acceptable to the government as a spokesman for the native population than the fiery archbishop.

The ANC and many of its supporters abroad feel that Buthelezi has betrayed the cause for personal power. "Gatsha Buthelezi, as head of a so-called 'homeland,' is part of the apartheid administration, answerable to the white minority," wrote the director of National Namibia Concerns, an antiapartheid organization based in the United States. "He is seen as an ambitious, unscrupulous man who for years has betrayed the freedom movement. . . . His army of trained thugs (Inkatha) has terrorized and murdered people for years."[1]

It was to a country torn with such factional dissension that the bishop-elect returned in 1985. His place in it was an uncertain one, but he remained firm in his faith. As he put it, "If you are doing God's work, then you jolly well believe it's His business to look after you." The days ahead were to hold much that would try that faith.

The new bishop's "enthronement"—his official inauguration—took place on February 4, 1985, with a ritual that combined the stately traditions of the Anglican church with the wailing chants of its African followers. Dressed in rich cream-and-red robes and wearing the peaked miter of his office, Tutu knocked three times at the west door of the cathedral with his bishop's staff, entered, and advanced solemnly up the aisle. From the high altar his voice rang out in the melodic cadences that have become known all over the world. Addressing a racially mixed audience of 1,500, Tutu repeated his familiar message, imploring the leaders of his country to understand the needs of its people. But this time there was a slight difference. Until now he had never actually advised a pullout of foreign investment—the ultimate economic pressure a foreign country could impose. He had made his position clear enough, but he had cautiously avoided expressing such a position directly, knowing that public support of such a withdrawal is illegal in South Africa, punishable by five years in prison. Now, from the bishop's throne of St. Mary's Cathedral, Tutu announced that he would risk legal action by advocating such a move "if apartheid is not actively dismantled in fourteen to eighteen months."

The bishop knew that he angered many people—even people in his own flock—by using the altar of his church as a platform for political pressure, but he had no doubt that he was doing the right thing. "We are accused of mixing politics with religion," he admitted, "but . . . what we do or say is based on our understanding of the Gospel of Jesus Christ. The God of the Bible is first encountered not in a religious setting but in an out-and-out political experience, in helping a rabble of slaves to escape from bondage."[2]

The office of bishop carries high privileges with it in Johannesburg. Tutu was assigned a large official residence in a wealthy white suburb and was entitled to membership in the exclusive—and exclusively white—Rand Country Club. But the new bishop preferred to remain in his smaller home in Soweto, and he courteously declined the chance to play golf with the business and social leaders of the city. In fact, as bishop of Johannesburg, Tutu was more in the thick of the fray than ever. He spoke from the pulpit and he spoke in the streets; he spoke in South Africa and he spoke abroad. He spoke wherever he could, and his public remained as passionately divided as ever. Foreign governments and institutions continued to shower him with awards and honorary degrees (in 1985 he earned five; the next two years, seven each), but he was vilified in his own country. Whites picketed his cathedral and plastered it with signs reading "Tutu—Devil in Church Clothing." The majority of South African newspapers attacked him at every opportunity, and the government issued warnings. But Tutu never held back, never retracted his statements.

In April, just two months after taking office, he first publicly defied the law by leading a procession of clergy through downtown Johannesburg to police headquarters. The traffic-stopping march was to protest the detention of an Anglican priest held for six months without charge. Riot police nervously surrounded the group. They could have arrested the bishop and his companions under the severe security laws, but the public mood was tense, and the police thought better of it. They contented themselves with photographing and videotaping the event and taking everyone's name as Tutu, wearing his purple cassock and carrying the golden crosier of his church, stood before the building and sang hymns with his fellow priests.

A few months later, Tutu put more than his freedom

on the line when he threw himself physically into a battle to save a man from an enraged crowd. The small black township of Duduza, thirty miles east of Johannesburg, had been the scene of a confrontation between police and protesters a week before, and the police had opened fire, killing ten people. The 40,000 residents of Duduza were in an angry mood.

Funerals were almost the only lawful gatherings for blacks, and they often turned into political demonstrations. On July 10, Bishop Tutu officiated at the funeral of four young men who had accidentally blown themselves up while attacking the home of someone they considered a collaborator with the white authorities. After the ceremony, the crowd turned violent as members of it accused a black man of being a government informer. They seized him, set his car afire, and prepared to throw him into the blaze.

Tutu, still dressed in his purple vestment, waded into the surging mob and pleaded with them. "This undermines the struggle," he cried as he shielded the man. Somehow he was able to pacify the angry crowd, and the frightened, bloodied man was taken to a hospital.

The bishop leads a funeral procession for victims of a clash with police. Since funerals were the only gatherings for blacks that were not unlawful, many were turned into political demonstrations.

Such incidents as this were becoming increasingly frequent. Finally, the alarmed government felt it had to clamp down still further to prevent a full-scale civil war. On July 20, 1985, a state of emergency was announced for thirty-six cities across South Africa. Under its provisions, the authorities (including policemen, soldiers, prison guards, and railway police) could search and arrest anyone and seize any property without a warrant and could use any force deemed necessary, "including force resulting in death," to do so. Suspects could be held indefinitely without trial or access to lawyers or family, and security officers were immune from prosecution or civil lawsuits for actions taken under the decree.

The state of emergency was declared on a Sunday. By that Thursday, 441 blacks had been arrested and 10 killed under its provisions, and by the end of the first month the arrests totaled over 1,500, the deaths more than 100. Four days after the state of emergency began, security forces raided the headquarters of the UDF while Tutu was addressing 25,000 mourners at yet another funeral. One week later, the government announced a ban on "political funerals."

Tutu's response was predictable. "I beg the authorities," he said the next day, "don't test us. I don't want to break the laws of this land, but if they pass laws which are quite unjust, quite intolerable, then I will break that law even if it means I have to go to jail."[3] Six days later, Tutu did openly break the new law to address another funeral of unrest victims. "I don't want to go to jail," he stated at that ceremony, "but if I am to go to jail for preaching the Gospel, then so be it."

He did not go to jail—the government could not risk a confrontation so dangerous as that—but the criticism of his behavior became more threatening as his speeches became more vehement, and the white authorities stepped up their campaign to discredit him and what he represents. The government of South Africa employed thirty-one U.S. public relations firms in 1983, according to an article in *Mother Jones*, giving "apartheid the most heavily endowed foreign propaganda machine in the United States. The four most active firms alone were paid a total of more than $1 million."[4]

The efforts of these firms have had some success. Many American conservatives oppose disinvestment as vigorously as the government in Pretoria does, and they consider Tutu a dangerous radical for supporting it. In August 1985, American television evangelist Jerry Falwell, the leader of the movement called the Moral Majority, made a five-day visit to South Africa and returned to report that the bishop was a "phony" for claiming to speak for the people of his country. Falwell later apologized, saying that he had used "an unfortunate choice of words," but he continued to urge Americans to support the South African government by investing in companies that do business with it.

The conservative position in the United States does not necessarily favor the racial policies of the South African government, but it fears that communism is the only alternative to them. "None of us conservatives support apartheid," argued fund-raiser Richard A. Viguerie. "The question is not whether they will have a white ruler or a black ruler in South Africa. They will have a white ruler for the foreseeable future. The question is whether that white ruler will be South African or Soviet. The alternative to the current government is a communist regime."[5]

The opposition to Tutu's position has not always taken such moderate form; some Americans have used stronger language about him than Falwell did. In June 1988, economist Donald S. McAlvany, president of a U.S. precious-metals firm and chairman of the Council on Southern Africa, told a business audience in Durban, South Africa, "Somebody ought to do something to stop [Tutu] from doing what he is doing. The man is a traitor. . . . The least you could do is remove the idiot's passport and not let him travel to our country, and somebody might want to even shoot him."[6]

So far, Tutu himself has escaped violence, but his family has not been left untouched. Mrs. Tutu was handcuffed and publicly humiliated over a traffic violation, and a more alarming incident occurred to the Tutus' son Trevor in August 1985. Trevor was attending a hearing in a Soweto courtroom for some of the 300 children arrested together for participating in the school boycott. White officers, armed with shotguns, began questioning an eight-year-old boy, and Trevor became so angry he called out an insult. He was promptly arrested and spent fourteen days in detention without charge.

Tutu continued to lead protest demonstrations despite the constant threat of arrest. At one potentially explosive Johannesburg funeral during the same month his son had been locked up, Tutu begged the police, "Please allow us to bury our dead with dignity. Please do not rub our noses in the dust. We are already hurt; we are already down. Don't trample on us. We are human beings; we are

*Leah Tutu often speaks out about
the problems in her country.*

not animals. And when we have a death, we cry like you cry."[7] His words of reconciliation worked. The police were even persuaded to provide buses to carry the mourners to the cemetery.

Tutu's defiance of laws he considered unjust did not always take such dramatic form. For example, he never carried his passbook. "It's just a small protest I make," he explained to a reporter in 1986.

I leave it at home. . . . I am contravening the law because the law is that every black person, male or female, from 16 to 60, must have the pass on his or her person. So if I took off my jacket, for example, and walked across the street . . . a policeman . . . has the right to arrest me. . . . Since they say a pass is only a form of identification, I have another form of identification that I carry. . . . It's a small protest just to indicate that I think it's ridiculous that persons should have such limitations placed on their freedom of movement in the land of their birth.[8]

In the midst of his political activities, Tutu did not neglect his pastoral duties, although sometimes they were made difficult and forced to take strange forms. One Sunday when he went to visit the banished Winnie Mandela to bring her Holy Communion, she was under house arrest and could not leave her yard from Friday night to Monday morning. So Bishop Tutu performed the ceremony over the fence around her house. "That is how she received Holy Communion," Tutu reported. "In Christian South Africa. Crazy. Crazy. I mean, really crazy."

The craziness of his country's policies did not move the American government to lend the support Tutu pleaded for, however, and he never ceased to reproach President Reagan for his refusal to impose economic and political pressure. A July 1986 speech by Reagan urging Congress to ignore the "emotional clamor" for sanctions enraged the bishop. He frankly told an American interviewer, "Your President is the pits as far as blacks are concerned," and later he said he found Reagan's speech "nauseating." Tutu was far from diplomatic. "The West, for my part, can go to hell," he stated. " . . . [Reagan] sits there like the great big white chief of old. [He thinks he] can tell us black people that we don't know what is good for us. The white man knows."[9]

Such blunt statements have alienated some of Tutu's admirers in the United States and earned him enemies. He has been not only tactless but often unreasonable in his charges. His accusation that the American government is "racist," for example, stung columnist William F. Buckley, Jr., to call him "reckless" and to say that his reasoning was "embarrassingly simpleminded." But despite the controversy that Tutu stirred up and the anger he aroused in his own country and abroad, his career advanced rapidly. Little more than a year after his enthronement as bishop of Johannesburg, his name was proposed for a higher title yet: that of the highest rank in the Anglican church in his country, the archbishop of Cape Town.

Again there were conflicts, both within the church and within the man himself. For Tutu, the election would mean once more leaving his home in Soweto, plucking his wife from her work directing the Domestic Workers and Employees' Project in Johannesburg, and moving away from his son Trevor, now married and a father himself and

working as an account executive with a Johannesburg advertising agency.

For the church, it meant placing at the helm a controversial figure whose provocative behavior, support of the ANC, and open plea for what the government called "economic sabotage" antagonized many. It also meant giving leadership of the church for the first time to a black man. It was a step more daring than some were prepared to take.

Tutu had been nominated before—in 1981—but the assembly of electors had not been ready for such a firebrand. By April 1986, however, the balance had shifted. Tutu was elected almost on the first ballot. Just twenty-five years after being ordained a priest of the Anglican church, Desmond Tutu assumed its highest office.

If Tutu had been defiant as a bishop, he became more so as an archbishop. Two months after his election, he joined a rent boycott in Soweto to protest apartheid, standing fast for over a year alongside Winnie Mandela and Ntatho Motlana, even after he was threatened with eviction from the home he keeps there. If anyone hoped that the high solemnity of his office would quiet him down and make him more cautious, they had once more misread the man.

Bishop Tutu has traveled all over the world speaking out against the South African system. Seen here with one of his daughters, Tutu leaves a rally in Newark, New Jersey.

As the ceremony of installation as archbishop approached, in fact, Tutu pressed his advantage and took full advantage of the attention his unique position brought him. He traveled to China and Japan, spreading his message as urgently as ever, and returned to face the usual newspaper charges of treason. Perhaps even more maddening to his opponents in South Africa were his preparations for the coming enthronement. He invited people from many countries, including American celebrities, to get as much propaganda exposure as he could from the event. In addition to civil rights advocates like Coretta Scott King, widow of slain leader Martin Luther King, Jr., and Sen. Edward M. Kennedy, Tutu asked such showbusiness personalities as singer Stevie Wonder and Harry Belafonte and Bill Cosby. "Clearly the Bishop intends to gain a great deal of political mileage out of his ecclesiastical superstardom," observed one South African newspaper angrily. "One thing is certain. There is no greater thorn in South Africa's side than this man of the cloth who strides through the world like a religious pop star."[10] That Tutu was a "thorn in South Africa's side" was intended to be an insult, but it may have been the greatest compliment his country's press could have given him.

There were white Anglicans who rejected their new black archbishop and left the church, but most supported him. The enthronement was more splendid even than the one in Johannesburg. The choir of St. George's Cathedral in Cape Town is world famous, and for this event it was supplemented by a choir from Soweto, which brought the audience to its feet with a traditional praise song usually sung at the enthronement of an African king.

Coretta Scott King, former Vice President George Bush, and Desmond Tutu lead the congregation at Ebenezer Baptist Church in Atlanta, Georgia, in singing "We Shall Overcome" during a service in honor of the late Dr. Martin Luther King, Jr., in 1986.

The ceremony was not conducted entirely in an atmosphere of unity and love, however. A white woman dressed in symbolic mourning placed a funeral wreath against the cathedral steps as a gesture of opposition, and demonstrators distributed anti-Tutu leaflets in front of the building. The state-run radio ignored the event completely, and no government official gave it any formal recognition by attending. But the new archbishop stressed his role as reconciler. Although he assured the 2,000 people crowding the hall that he would not stop calling for justice even if it meant his arrest, he repeated his plea for a nonviolent approach to the problems of their country. Somewhat to the surprise of many, he did not condemn the state president. "Whether I like it or not," Tutu said, "whether he likes it or not, P. W. Botha is my brother, and I must desire and pray for the best for him."[11]

Tutu realized the dangers and responsibilities of his new post. A week after his enthronement, he recounted, "I got a telegram congratulating me on my 'enthornment.' Sometimes I think that's really the right word."[12] If he was a "thorn in South Africa's side," he knew that the path before him was to be no less thorny.

The first problem he faced in his new position was where to live. The official residence, called Bishopscourt, is, of course, in a white area, and the church must ask for

Archbishop Tutu blesses
the city of Cape Town
following his enthronement
as archbishop.

special permission for its black leader to live there. This Tutu refuses to do, as he does not recognize the law forbidding him to live in a "white" area. He prefers to live illegally at Bishopscourt.

Defying the law has become a regular procedure for Tutu, and for all of its bluster, the government is obviously reluctant to risk the international outrage that would result if it took action. As a British magazine put it when the archbishop deliberately violated a new law against publicly calling for the release of detainees in 1987, "On some toes, South African policemen do not put their big boots."[13] Instead of arresting Tutu, the government hastily redefined the law, explaining that it did not refer to church services.

Tutu's luck, and the government's caution, could not last forever, however. On February 24, 1988, Pretoria announced its harshest crackdown since the banning of the ANC and the PAC during the Soweto riots of 1960. The government outlawed seventeen antiapartheid organizations, including the UDF, and prohibited labor unions from all political action.

Tutu responded at once, stating that the move "amounts to a declaration of war." Those who want change, he said, "are being encouraged by the government's actions to turn to violence. White South Africans must realize that we are at a crossroads. If they don't stop this government soon, and there's not much hope that they will, we are heading for war."[14] When he and other clergymen, including Dr. Allan Boesak, took to the streets to protest the new decree, they were all arrested.

They were detained only briefly, but the government had proved that it meant business and trusted that it had intimidated the opposition. Tutu was not intimidated, however. A few weeks later, in March, he organized a new group, the Committee for the Defense of Democracy, to replace the UDF. The government banned it immediately, taking special care to ban the first meeting specifically. The language of the decree could not be misunderstood: the committee was prohibited from engaging in "any activities whatsoever."

The Committee for the Defense of Democracy did not survive, but Tutu made a point with it. He dramatized to other countries how his government worked. "It is clear to me, as it must be to everyone in the world," he announced, "that we are dealing with a government here that is virtually totalitarian and determined to bludgeon God's people into submission." He called on President Reagan and British prime minister Margaret Thatcher, both of whom still refused to support his call for economic sanctions, to observe what was going on in South Africa. He demanded to know what more proof they needed that they were cooperating with a government that "will tolerate no opposition to its evil and immoral policies." His message was at once a plea and a warning. "We refuse to be treated as a doormat for people to wipe their jackboots on," he concluded his statement. "We refuse to be manipulated into a position of oppression."[15]

Allan Boesak, who had participated with Tutu in forming the committee, was more defiant yet: "The South African government has signed its own death warrant," he pronounced. "No government can take on the living God and survive."[16]

President Botha responded on March 16 to this theological threat with a warning—supported by the DRC—

that Tutu was "distorting the true message of Christ" by bringing the Church into the political arena. It was a point Tutu had heard before, from the government and from members of his own church, and he was ready for it. In fact, he rather welcomed the opportunity to address the subject publicly. He replied to Botha with a 3,200-word letter citing no fewer than thirty Biblical passages to show that his involvement with national affairs was consistent with his religious calling. "The Bible teaches quite un-equivocally that people are created for fellowship, for to-getherness," he wrote, "not for alienation, apartness, enmity, and division."

He went on to give examples of religious figures from both the Old and the New Testament—Isaiah, Elijah, Na-than, Jesus, and the Apostles—who had defied political authority. When questioned by reporters in New York, where he was visiting to receive the Albert Schweitzer Humanitarian Award, Tutu said, "I think President Botha wanted to show us he was taking us on, not on the basis of politics but on our own grounds." He was clearly en-joying the publicity. "The South African government pro-vided us with a platform we wouldn't have otherwise had for preaching the Gospel,"[17] he observed with satisfaction.

The conflict over apartheid continues to be more than a theological one, however, and it shows little sign of diminishing. If anything, it has become increasingly bitter, dividing the country into warring camps. In June 1988, the government of South Africa extended its two-year-old state of emergency in an effort to suppress the growing protest against its policies. More alarming yet, a series of bombings and arson attacks against the offices of anti-apartheid groups has rocked the country for the past few

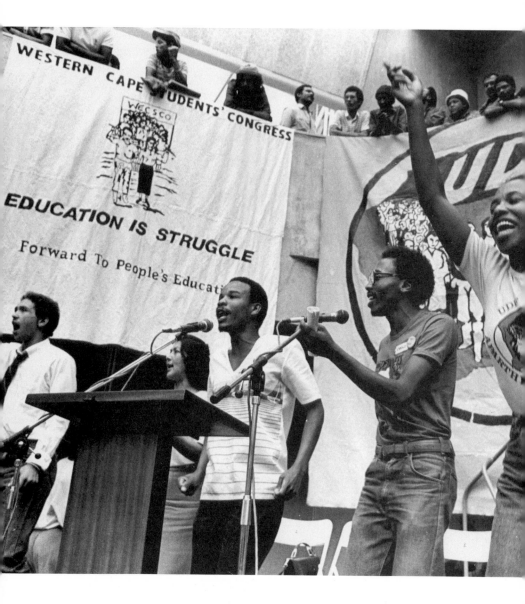

*Protests and rallies by both students (above)
and workers (over) go on unabated
as the struggle continues in South Africa.*

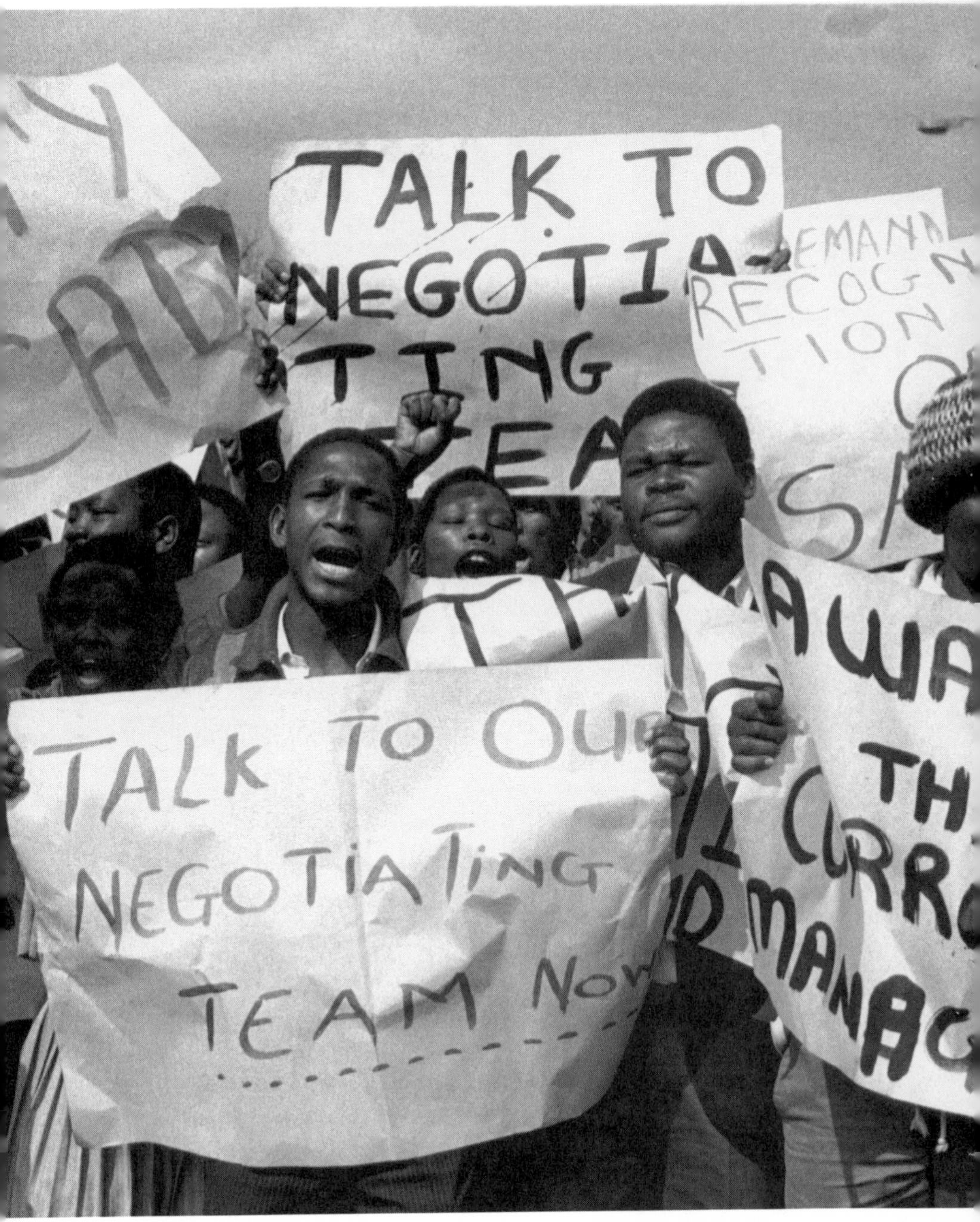
TALK TO
NEGOTIA-
TING
RECOGN
TION
TALK TO
NEGOTIATING
TEAM

years. The offices of the Congress of South African Trade Unions (COSATU), the largest black labor federation in the country, were destroyed in 1987, and in August 1988, a massive explosion wrecked Khotso House, the headquarters of the SACC and several other church groups in Johannesburg. "We have no doubt that this act was committed by the perpetrators or supporters of apartheid," Tutu stated grimly. "The South African Council of Churches has long been the target of the enemies of peace."[18]

The issue of foreign sanctions as a means of resolving the conflict continues to rage, too, both in South Africa and in the United States. The respected legislator Helen Suzman, a warm personal friend of Tutu's (she accompanied him and his family on a picnic the day before his enthronement as archbishop of Cape Town), remains firmly opposed to disinvestment, as does Gatsha Buthelezi, but the idea has won increasing support in the United States. In 1986 a bill imposing limited economic sanctions against South Africa was passed over President Reagan's veto, and a stronger one is under consideration.

The 1986 law prohibits new investment, new bank loans, oil and arms exports, and imports of agricultural products, uranium, iron, steel, and Krugerrands. Opponents of new, stronger legislation argue that the 1986 sanctions have done nothing to bring about an end to apartheid and that, in fact, the political and social situation in South Africa is worse than it was before. Those who support additional sanctions point out, as Tutu has repeatedly observed, that the United States has not held back from imposing restrictions on Russia, Poland, Cuba, Nicaragua, Libya, and Panama even when these restrictions have not shown any immediate results.

In September 1988, a new and far more sweeping bill was approved in the U.S. Senate Foreign Relations Committee, prohibiting "the purchase, acquisition, ownership, or holding by any American individual or entity of any investment in South Africa."[19] A similar bill was passed by the House of Representatives in August 1988. These bills were hotly disputed in the United States and watched nervously in South Africa.

Whatever the future of this controversial legislation, the most certain evidence that Tutu's efforts at discouraging U.S. investment in South Africa have begun to succeed has been the withdrawal of business already there. One hundred and sixty companies—about half of the U.S. firms in South Africa—have ceased operation there since 1983. As one market analyst observes, "The flight of foreign capital . . . erodes business confidence and reduces new investment."[20] So it may be that Tutu's goal will be achieved even without the United States imposing economic sanctions.

In the midst of all the uncertainty and upheaval of his country, meanwhile, Desmond Tutu remains basically optimistic and very busy. His day begins early. He gets up at 5:00 A.M. and says his prayers. He used to jog every morning, but now uses an exercise bicycle before he performs his first church duty of the day, a six o'clock mass for parishioners who must go to work early. His day is full of meetings, interviews, conferences, and public appearances, but there is always time for prayer and meditation. When his schedule permits, he goes on a solitary retreat, as he has done ever since he was in school.

Of the future he has no doubt whatever. He is aware that he is personally in danger, but he is reconciled to it.

Despite a hectic schedule of meetings, interviews, conferences, and church duties, the Archbishop of South Africa continues to protest, like at this rally to salute jailed leader Nelson Mandela on his seventieth birthday.

"If they are after you," he says, "they are after you. And if they want to assassinate you, they'll assassinate you. . . . If you begin worrying about that, then you might as well stay home and sleep."[21] Tutu hopes only that he will live to see his country free, as he is absolutely certain it will be, "not because we are good," he explains, "not because we deserve it, but because God is God."[22]

In that free South Africa he knows is coming, Desmond Tutu sees no political future for himself. "I will be a pastor," he insists. "That is what I want. I am quite clear in my mind." The future president of South Africa, for Tutu, is unquestionably Nelson Mandela. "I said to Winnie," he recalls, " 'Go and get that husband of yours out of jail, woman, and tell him that he is making me do the work that he ought to be doing.' "[23]

However he sees himself—as pastor or politician— Desmond Tutu remains the conscience of his nation, an example to the world of courage and faith—faith in God and faith in a South Africa in which everyone will be equal. He knows it will come, he explains, "because all of us— black and white together—are of infinite worth, since we are made in the image of God. And all of us—black and white together—are made for freedom."[24]

CHRONOLOGY

Oct. 7, 1931   Born to Zachariah and Aletta Tutu in Klerksdorp, Transvaal, South Africa

1951–53   Attended Bantu Normal College, Pretoria; received teacher's certificate, 1953

1954   Received B.A., University of South Africa; taught at Western High School, Sophiatown, Johannesburg

1955   Married Leah Nomalizo Shenxane; taught at Munsieville High School, Krugersdorp

1958–60   Attended St. Peter's Theological College, Rosettenville, Johannesburg; received L.Th., ordained deacon; served at St. Alban's Church, in Benoni, Transvaal, 1960

1961   Ordained an Anglican priest; served in Thokoza

1962–66   Attended King's College, London, England; served as part-time curate, St. Alban's Church, London, 1962; St. Mary's Church, in Bletchingley, Surrey, England, received B.Th., 1965; received M.Th., 1966

1967   Taught at St. Peter's, Federal Theological Seminary, Alice, Ciskei, South Africa; served as chaplain, Ft. Hare University, in Alice

1969   Taught at University of Botswana, Lesotho, and Swaziland, in Roma, Lesotho

1972–75	Served as associate director, Theological Education Fund, in Bromley, Kent, England
1975	Appointed dean of Johannesburg
1976	Elected bishop of Lesotho
1978	Appointed secretary-general, South African Council of Churches
1984	Received Nobel Peace Prize; elected bishop of Johannesburg
1986	Elected archbishop of Cape Town

SOURCE NOTES

Chapter 1

1. Address accepting the Albert Schweitzer Humanitarian Award, the Riverside Church, New York City, April 29, 1988.
2. *Rand Daily Mail*, South Africa, October 12, 1979.
3. *Cape Times*, South Africa, April 20, 1981.
4. Quoted in Colin and Margaret Legum, *The Bitter Choice: Eight South Africans' Resistance to Tyranny*, Cleveland: World, 1968, p. 22.
5. Address at a Home and Family Life Conference, Hammanskraal, South Africa, March 2, 1979, quoted in Desmond Tutu, *Crying in the Wilderness*, p. 121.
6. *London Observer*, May 8, 1983.
7. *The Other Side*, January/February 1985.
8. Ibid.
9. Ibid.
10. Ibid.

Chapter 2

1. *Washington Post Magazine*, February 16, 1986.
2. Mmutlanyane Stanley Mogoba, "From Munsieville to Oslo," in Buti Tlhagale and Itumeleng Mosala, eds., *Hammering Swords Into Ploughshares*, p. 24.
3. Shirley du Boulay, *Tutu: Voice of the Voiceless*, p. 40.

4. *Washington Post Magazine*, February 16, 1986.
5. Trevor Huddleston, *Naught for Your Comfort*, p. 157.

Chapter 3

1. *The Episcopalian*, January 1986.
2. *London Observer*, May 8, 1983.
3. *South African Outlook*, February 1982.
4. *The Other Side*, January/February 1985.
5. *King's College Newsletter*, London, December, 1984.

Chapter 4

1. Shirley du Boulay, *Tutu: Voice of the Voiceless*, p. 92.
2. *Ecunews*, June 1983.
3. *The Episcopalian*, January 1986.

Chapter 5

1. *The Episcopalian*, January 1986.
2. *Sunday Tribune*, South Africa, May 6, 1976; reprinted in Desmond Tutu, *Hope and Suffering*, pp. 28–36.
3. *South African Outlook*, February 1982.
4. "Steve Biko—A Tribute," oration at the funeral of Steve Biko, September 1977; reprinted in Desmond Tutu, *Hope and Suffering*, pp. 61–64.

Chapter 6

1. *Rand Daily Mail*, South Africa, October 12, 1979.
2. *Christian Science Monitor*, November 28, 1979.
3. Desmond Tutu, address at the United Nations, March 23, 1981.
4. *Cape Times*, South Africa, February 22, 1980.
5. Desmond Tutu, testimony before the Eloff Commission; quoted in du Boulay, *Tutu: Voice of the Voiceless*, pp. 174–75.
6. Michael Sovern, commencement address, Columbia University, New York, N.Y., May 18, 1982.

Chapter 7

1. *The Star*, South Africa, April 15, 1985.
2. *Washington Post*, June 25, 1983.
3. *New York Times*, December 11, 1983.
4. *The Sunday Times*, Cape Town, South Africa, October 21, 1984.

Chapter 8

1. Solveig Kjeseth, letter to *Rocky Mountain News*, Denver, Colorado, November 11, 1985.
2. Desmond Tutu, enthronement charge, St. Mary's Cathedral, Johannesburg, South Africa, February 3, 1985; quoted in *New York Times*, February 4, 1985.
3. *Washington Post*, August 7, 1985.
4. Greg Goldin, *Mother Jones*, January 1985.
5. Richard A. Viguerie, quoted in *New York Times*, August 21, 1985.
6. *The New Nation*, Johannesburg, South Africa, August 21, 1985.
7. *Newsweek*, August 19, 1985.
8. *The Episcopalian*, January 1986.
9. *New York Post*, July 23, 1986.
10. *The Citizen*, South Africa; quoted in *New York Times*, August 22, 1986.
11. *Financial Times*, England, September 8, 1986.
12. *New Republic*, October 27, 1986.
13. *The Economist*, England, April 18, 1987.
14. *New York Times*, February 25, 1988.
15. *New York Times*, March 13, 1988.
16. *New York Times*, March 14, 1988.
17. *New York Times*, May 3, 1988.
18. *The Washington Post*, September 1, 1988.
19. *New York Times*, September 15, 1988.
20. Merle Lipton, quoted in *New York Times*, June 12, 1988.
21. *Rolling Stone*, November 21, 1985.
22. *Washington Post*, February 16, 1986.
23. *Life*, November 1985.
24. Desmond Tutu, "The Education of Free Men," in Mark H. Uhlig, ed., *Apartheid in Crisis*, p. 30.

BIBLIOGRAPHY

Davis, Stephen M. *Apartheid's Rebels: Inside South Africa's Hidden War*. New Haven, Conn.: Yale University Press, 1987. An exciting account of the underground struggle against apartheid in South Africa.

de Gruchy, John, and Villa-Vicencio, Charles, eds. *Apartheid Is a Heresy*. Grand Rapids, Mich.: William B. Eerdmans, 1983. A collection of theological essays arguing that apartheid is against the teachings of the Bible.

du Boulay, Shirley. *Tutu: Voice of the Voiceless*. Grand Rapids, Mich.: William B. Eerdmans, 1988. The authorized biography, a detailed history of the man and his work against a background of his country and his church.

Harrison, David. *The White Tribe of Africa*. Berkeley, Cal.: University of California Press, 1981. The history of the Afrikaners' rise to power, giving an explanation of their attitudes and their defense of apartheid.

Huddleston, Trevor. *Naught for Your Comfort*. New York: Doubleday, 1962. The pioneering attack on apartheid, still prophetic and moving.

Lapping, Brian. *Apartheid, a History*. New York: Braziller, 1986. A detailed examination of the complex problems of apartheid.

Leach, Graham. *South Africa: No Easy Path to Peace*. London: Routledge & Kegan Paul, 1986. An in-depth study of the racial problems of South Africa.

Lelyveld, Joseph. *Move Your Shadow: South Africa Black and White.* New York: New York Times Books, 1985. Perhaps the leading modern presentation, by a *New York Times* reporter. Insightful and authoritative.

Tlhagale, Buti, and Itumeleng Mosala, eds. *Hammering Swords Into Ploughshares: Essays in Honor of Archbishop Desmond Mpilo Tutu.* Grand Rapids, Mich.: William B. Eerdmans, 1987. A collection of personal tributes, theological essays, and background material by Tutu's associates and colleagues. Some of it is highly technical.

Tutu, Desmond. *Crying in the Wilderness: The Struggle for Justice in South Africa.* Grand Rapids, Mich.: William B. Eerdmans, 1982. Tutu's sermons, speeches, articles, and press releases from 1978 to 1980, when he was the leader of the South African Council of Churches, each with an explanatory headnote. Includes many moving personal glimpses.

————. *Hope and Suffering.* Grand Rapids, Mich.: William B. Eerdmans, 1984. A collection of Tutu's sermons and speeches, beginning with his 1976 "Open Letter" to Prime Minister Vorster.

Uhlig, Mark H. ed. *Apartheid in Crisis.* New York: Vintage Books, 1986. A collection of astute and timely essays by a wide variety of experts (including Desmond Tutu) on the current state of race relations in South Africa.

INDEX

ABOUT THE AUTHOR

Dennis Wepman is a free-lance writer who has written on sociology, popular culture, and black folklore and used to teach English at Queens College.

Among his books are biographies of Jomo Kenyatta, Simon Bolivar, Adolf Hitler, and Helen Keller.

Mr. Wepman lives in New York City.